ASA's guide to

GETTING PUBLISHED

Understanding and navigating Australia's book industry

Juliet Rogers

AUSTRALIAN SOCIETY *of* AUTHORS

Proudly published by the Australian Society of Authors 2022
Suite C1.06, 22-36 Mountain Street, ULTIMO NSW 2007
www.asauthors.org

Cover design by David Potter
Typeset in Australia by transformer.com.au
Printed and bound in Australia by Pegasus Media & Logistics

ISBN: 978-0-9592819-0-3 (Australian edition)

A catalogue record for this book is available from the National Library of Australia.

This publication has been assisted by the Australian Government through the Australia Council for the Arts, its arts funding and advisory body.

About the author

Juliet Rogers has spent her career in the book industry, working across every sector including bookselling, publishing and author advocacy. She was Managing Director of Random House in both New Zealand and Australia, followed by 10 years as CEO of Murdoch Books. She then set up her own small publishing and consultancy business, *The Wild Colonial Company* before taking up the reins as CEO of the ASA from 2016 to 2020. Juliet has also held the roles of Chair of Booksellers New Zealand, President of the Australian Publishers Association and was the inaugural chair of the industry's charity, The Indigenous Literacy Foundation. She is currently Managing Director and Publisher at Echo Publishing.

This varied experience has allowed her to gain insight into the challenges and opportunities that face all the key players in the industry.

About the ASA

The Australian Society of Authors has been the national peak professional association, community and voice of Australia's writers and illustrators since it was established in 1963. Our purpose is to support authors and illustrators to pursue sustainable creative careers through our advocacy, professional development, resources, support and advice. We hope this book helps to answer one of the most common questions posed to the ASA: how do I get published?

Contents

INTRODUCTION

Introduction

In my four years at the Australian Society of Authors (ASA), hardly a day went by without at least one prospective author seeking advice on how to get published, and it's easy to understand why. The industry is complex and can be difficult to navigate, with rules and etiquette that are opaque to the uninitiated. Spoiled for choice, publishers and literary agents are closing their doors to unsolicited manuscripts, further narrowing access for authors, particularly first timers. And even for those lucky enough to secure a deal, advances are shrinking, and there's an increasing expectation that they will actively market and support their publication.

As the large multinational publishers grow ever bigger, so too do the handful of mega authors who increasingly dominate the bestseller list. This, in turn, drives publishers towards books that follow the trends set by those stellar bestsellers, to try and reduce their risk.

Social media and global retailers have further ramped up this phenomenon, so that hand-selling by independent retailers is being overtaken by internet retailers, where brand authors flourish.

But the basics stay the same. The publishing pattern has always looked something like this:

SALES PATTERN

If 20,000 books are published per year:

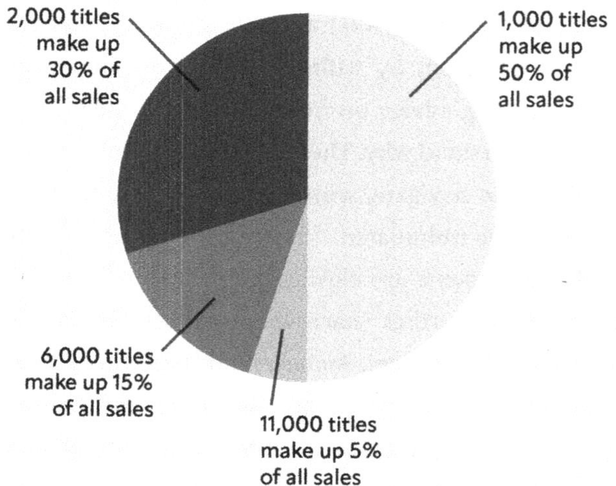

Although the percentages on this chart are educated guesses, what's important is the relationship between the sales revenue and the number of titles in each category. Of course, we hear much about the enormous sales of such titles as *Boy Swallows Universe* by Trent Dalton, and this fuels the dream of international stardom for many aspiring authors. These titles, however, have always been few and far between, and a mixture of talent, timing and luck lies behind their success. Publishers can rarely predict this, as evidenced by the very small print run for the first *Harry Potter* book, but they are very adept at riding the wave when it first starts to develop.

Publishing is an ecosystem, in which each category of title has its role. The tiny number of runaway successes may make up a disproportionately large proportion of the total sales value, but backlist titles, those publications that go on to sell steadily for many years, are as vital to the industry as the showy bestsellers. Many authors have created a loyal readership without ever appearing on a bestseller list and have built a sustainable career doing what they love most.

The market is crowded and fiercely competitive, but new technology, the growth in social media and the ever-changing media and entertainment landscape have also broadened the opportunities for authors:

- Self-publishing has become a viable and affordable option, particularly in certain genres

- Social media can help writers to build a community around their work, which can entice publisher interest

- The exponential growth of audiobooks in recent years has helped make their production more accessible and affordable

- The rise in streaming services on television has opened a new market for writers, many of whom are now writing directly for screen, rather than waiting for a published book to pique a producer's interest

- There's an increased interest in writers of diverse cultures and experiences

- There's growing enthusiasm for different forms of expression, including poetry and short stories, particularly if you've already established an audience.

Achieving publication is still not easy, particularly when most writers work in isolation, but no one knows this better than the ASA team. Because they have worked with thousands of writers, they understand the challenges you face and your uncertainty about where to even start. They share your joy when you receive your first contract and your despair when your work has been rejected and, above all, they understand that knowledge is power.

This guide is designed to give you the tools and information that will allow you to confidently plan your path towards publication. Whether you're an unpublished writer dreaming of the day when you finally hold your own book, or a published author whose career has floundered, this realistic, practical advice on both traditional publishing and self-publishing is designed to give you the very best chance of success.

Remember, success is a matter of perception. If you're convinced that you'll feel the thrill of achievement only if your book hits No. 1 on the bestseller list, chances are that you're destined for disappointment. But if you focus on the joy of writing and perfecting your craft, even if publication remains elusive, no one can take that away from you.

Samuel Johnson claimed that only a fool writes for anything but money, but most of the writers I've known write for a myriad other reasons. Primarily because it brings them deep pleasure and immense satisfaction:

> *'Here's the rough-and-tumble fact of it: The overwhelming odds are that when you're writing your first book (and even your second) you will be writing it for free, you will not receive a contract or advance from a major publisher, and you will not get an agent. I say this with utmost affection and empathy. I also say, let the statistical truth of all that, free us to write what we love, what we want to write, exactly what we would write for free. And once you're dancing down that path, write hard, write the thing the best you can write it, and who knows? Maybe the phone ringing on your bedside*

table is that literary agent and they're calling with good news. Best of all they're calling because they love your work as much as you do. And if that call doesn't come through, not right away, where does that leave you? With no regrets. All respect to Dr Johnson, [but] the far, far better quote (for my 'money') is: 'Never for money, always for love...' Talking Heads. They didn't just write it. They sang it.'

Ruuf Wangersen, author

Although determination, fortitude, luck, hard work and, above all, talent play their part, no one path can guarantee publishing success. But if you build your knowledge of the industry, plan carefully, listen to feedback from the right people and continually hone your writing skills, you can improve the odds significantly. Never forget, however, that the one thing that you never have to lose, is the joy of writing.

• • •

The guide is arranged in five parts, moving from the big picture landscape of the industry and how it works, through to the specifics of publishing and how you can best equip yourself for success. Part 1 provides all the information you need about the publishing industry and process so that you can make an informed decision about the right path to take. It applies to *all* authors and illustrators in trade publishing. Part 2 looks at what to expect in a traditional publishing arrangement, while Part 3 takes you down the self-publishing route. Part 4 lists ways in which you can supplement your income and Part 5 contains a useful list of industry organisations.

PART 1

PART 1

So you want to be an author

Let's start by exploring the book industry. We'll concentrate on Australia, since that is likely to be your primary market, but it's also useful to have an overview of how Australian books with international sales potential reach markets around the world.

The Australian book market

SALES DATA

Let's begin by defining what market we're talking about. Publishing is broken down into three broad categories:

1. *Trade:* general books that are bought by consumers, from online or bricks and mortar bookstores.
2. *Educational:* books that are published for the educational market from primary school through

to tertiary education, often in accordance with the state or national school curriculum.

3. *Scholarly and academic:* works often published as articles in journals or as books by university presses.

Both educational and academic publishing have their own specialist requirements, which aren't covered in this guide. Our concern is trade publishing, across all genres of books intended for a general audience.

It's not easy to find reliable statistics on the size of the book market in Australia, but according to Nielsen BookScan, there were 22,634 new titles published in 2019, based on the number of ISBNs (international standard book numbers) issued by Thorpe Bowker. Although these titles were produced by 5,564 different publishing entities, 90% of which were self-published authors, bringing out between one and five titles a year. At the other end of the scale, 20 publishers produced more than 100 titles (a big drop from the 31 publishers in 2018), 115 produced between 20 and 99 titles and a further 155 publishers between two and five books.

Only 400 or so of all these new titles sold more than 10,000 copies and between January and August 2020, the Top 10 bestseller list for Australian books was dominated by *Bluey* publications, which filled seven of those top slots.

The publishing industry pie chart based on these statistics would therefore look very similar to the sales chart in the introduction, with a small number of publishers producing the lion's share of the sales revenue, but not the number of titles.

PUBLISHERS

The Australian publishing landscape can be a little complex, but we'll start the demystification process by discussing some of the terminology that may be new to you.

Publisher: This term can be confusing, because it's used to refer to both the company that produces the books (e.g. HarperCollins) and the person within the company who acquires and produces new books for the program.

Distributor: This is the warehouse company that receives the print books, processes orders from bookshops, despatches the books and handles the returns. There are three major warehouses in Australia: Alliance Distribution Services (ADS), owned by Hachette, Harper Entertainment Distribution Services (HEDS), owned by HarperCollins, and United Book Distributors (UBD) owned by Penguin Random House. All these large warehouses manage the distribution for multiple publishers, for an agreed percentage of the sales each publisher generates.

Confusingly, however, many smaller publishers that don't have their own sales team also use the term 'distributor' to describe the company that handles their sales into stores. That company, in turn, will have their own agreement with a warehouse and will manage both the sales and distribution for the small publisher. For example, New South Books (NSB) has its own publishing list, but also manages the sales and distribution for some smaller publishers, such as CSIRO Publishing, using their own NSB sales force and distributing the physical books through their agreement with the ADS warehouse.

Agency: An agency is an international publishing list that is represented in the Australian market by another publisher. For instance, Allen & Unwin (A&U) have a number of agencies, including Faber & Faber, a well-established British independent publishing company. A&U buys books from Faber & Faber and then sells, markets and distributes those titles on Faber's behalf, in the Australian market.

BOOKSELLERS

We'll now move on to the booksellers to whom all the publishers sell. It's important to understand the composition of the Australian retail book market so that you can work out where your book is likely to sell best.

Independent bookstores

Unlike the other major English-language book markets, Australia is fortunate to have preserved a healthy independent bookshop sector – more than 150 high-quality stores – in the face of such challenges as the growth of Amazon, the rise of eBooks and the diversification of mixed-retail outlets stocking books. Independent stores are almost always owner-operated and the owner or buyer is the person who selects which books to stock and in what numbers. As a result, the stock range in these stores is often broader and more eclectic than in a chain store. Some independents also belong to buying collectives, which allows them to buy key titles as a group and secure better buying terms from the publisher.

These shops are a vital part of the industry because the passionate people who own and staff them champion authors. They're the ones who start the word of mouth and actively sell to their dedicated customers. Debut books, literary fiction and thoughtful non-fiction often begin their lives in this sector of the market, where personal recommendations from the staff are an important aspect of the shop's marketing strategy.

Some independent bookshops may also stock a small number of self-published titles by local authors on consignment, and many host book launches and welcome authors for in-store signings.

Bookshop chains

There has been a significant diminishment in this sector of the market, due to the collapse of both the Angus & Robertson and Borders chains some 10 years ago. The most significant of these is QBD with more than 80 stores, all company owned, followed by the Dymocks franchise chain which is still a key player with some 60 stores, followed by Collins Booksellers' 23 stores and then a number of smaller owner-operated groups including Readings, Berkelouw and Harry Hartog, which still sit within the independent grouping. Although each of these groups operates differently, they all consolidate their major new title orders in order to optimise their buying terms with the publishers. Their backlist ranges, however, remain broad and individual.

Book chains will champion new authors, but more often those already being strongly supported by their publisher with marketing and publicity. Like the indies, the book chain stores try to emphasise range to their customers as a way of differentiating themselves from the mass market outlets.

Discount department stores

This sector is primarily represented by Big W, Kmart and Target. Thanks to their investment in a very experienced and respected book buyer, Big W is currently the leader of the group for the publishing industry.

These stores focus on large-volume sales of a narrow range of commercial titles, for both adults and children. They have a very small backlist offering and all the purchasing is managed by the one head office buyer. They heavily discount the big new title releases, which means that Big W alone can sell as much as 30% of a major mass market title.

Online retailers

Online retailers can stock a significantly higher number of titles than a bricks and mortar store, partly because they don't have the same physical constraints, but also because print on demand and the capacity to hold very small amounts of stock allows them to carry a much wider range of titles.

Booktopia is an Australian-owned online book retailer

with a very extensive range of titles. As at February 2021, it claims a 15% share of book online sales and 6% of total book sales in Australia.

Amazon Australia launched to little fanfare at the end of 2017. Although not yet dominant in book sales in this market, it certainly dominates the sales of eBooks in the US and UK (83% and 88% market share respectively) and the launch of a local print-on-demand facility in 2021 leaves little doubt that Amazon's significance in the Australian retail market will soon grow.

Many of the independent retail outlets have an online presence, as does Dymocks, but online sales currently represent a very small percentage of their overall revenue.

Specialist wholesalers

In addition to stores either focused primarily on books, or mixed retailers with a significant book offering, there are more specialist retail opportunities for niche genres and categories of books that publishers reach by working through wholesalers. These include, but are not limited to, children's, gift books and libraries.

Children's: Scholastic is a specialist children's book publisher that sells to the bookshop network outlined above but also markets their list and lists from other publishers, into several niche areas:

- Book Clubs, which is a catalogue of curated titles distributed through a wide network of schools

- Book fairs, where children can select their own books from a range of titles
- Australian Standing Orders, which is a subscription service to school libraries, offering the best new releases from all publishers, together with comprehensive teachers' notes which provide ideas for classroom activities and discussion.

Although books made available through these initiatives are sold to Scholastic at a high discount, these additional sales help publishers to reach an economic print run level and provide authors with valuable exposure across a broad range of Australian schools.

There is also a network of educational wholesalers who will stock key children's reading books alongside educational texts and equipment.

Gift books: Publishers will also sell certain books to gift wholesalers, who distribute and market a wide variety of products into specialist gift outlets. Lifestyle illustrated titles and classic children's picture books are of particular appeal.

Libraries: Throughout the country libraries purchase their stock via a network of specialist wholesalers, who deliver print titles to libraries 'shelf ready', meaning that protective covers and catalogue numbers have already been applied. For popular fiction and children's books in particular, these sales can provide valuable additional revenue for publishers and authors alike.

HOW DOES THE SALES PROCESS WORK?

We'll go into the sales process in more detail when we examine how the publishing industry works, but regardless of their size, all publishers have the same fundamental purpose: to produce their own titles and sell these, and any other publishing lists they represent, to booksellers. If we correlate this with other industries, the publishers are the wholesalers, since they don't sell directly to the public, other than some small sales that they make from their own websites. This means that the bookseller is the person the publisher needs to convince to buy their books.

In Australia, new titles are released on a monthly cycle and some of the big publishers may have hundreds of new titles being released every month. All medium to large traditional publishers have a sales force, comprising either their own salaried sales representatives, 'reps', or a commission sales team linked to their distributor. These reps show book buyers their range of monthly new titles and help them to select the most appropriate titles for their store.

To complicate matters further, international sales work differently from sales within Australia. With the exception of eBooks sold by global online retailers, international sales are made between publishers in one of three ways:

1. ***Distribution:*** Some Australian publishers have distribution agreements with publishers in other markets, primarily Britain and the US. This means that the international publisher sells, markets and distributes the Australian publisher's titles within

their own market, similar to the agency selling discussed earlier, only in reverse.

2. ***Rights sale:*** In this scenario, the Australian publisher licenses the copyright in a book to an international publisher, in specific languages or territories. For example, a book can be licensed to a Spanish publisher for the Spanish language in the Spanish territory only, or that publisher can be licensed for the Spanish language worldwide, allowing them to sell the Spanish edition in any Spanish-speaking country in the world. That publisher signs an agreement with the Australian publisher, pays an advance and royalty, somewhat like an author contract, and then translates the work if necessary and produces the book under their own imprint, in the format and at the price best suited to their market.

3. ***Co-edition:*** In this type of sale, the Australian publisher sells a volume quantity of a book to an international publisher and then prints for that publisher, simply changing the publisher details on the spine and imprint page and, sometimes, the cover. The physical books are then shipped to the international publisher directly from the printer. If the sale is to a foreign language publisher, that publisher will supply the translated text and the Australian publisher will then send those files to the printer. This type of sale is more common in

illustrated books, as production costs are much higher than text publishing, and so it's an advantage for both publishers to reduce the per unit cost of the print price by increasing the size of the print run, as they print all co-editions together.

Book fairs play an important role in securing these deals, particularly the 'big three' of London, Frankfurt and Bologna (children's books only), but Australian publishers are also starting to spread their net wider, particularly in Asia. According to 2021 research conducted by Macquarie University, China is a rapidly growing export market for Australian books. Medium to large publishers will likely send their own staff, either a specialist rights sale person or a publisher, to attend these fairs and manage all the follow-up, but smaller publishers may appoint agents specialising in certain territories, who will sell on their behalf, or prospect for likely titles.

That brings us to the final area of international publishing, buy-ins, which is the reverse of rights sales. The Australian publisher will buy in a title from an international publisher, either by way of a rights deal or co-edition purchase, and then sell that book in this market under their own imprint.

How does the publishing industry work?

Now let's turn our attention to how the publishing industry operates.

KEY PLAYERS

Literary agent

A literary agent is a person with skills, knowledge and experience in the publishing industry, who represents you, the author, to the publisher and acts as the go-between with the publisher. Their purpose is to manage the business side of your writing career, leaving you free to focus on the creative side.

Publisher/commissioning editor

This is the person within the publishing company who is responsible for the acquisition of new authors. In a small publishing company they will most likely run the business but, in a larger concern, they will head up the editorial and production teams: the people who turn your manuscript into a book.

A good publisher keeps in touch with the market, understanding and, ideally, predicting trends, identifies and develops good writing, regardless of genre, reads widely, communicates effectively and can see opportunities where others see none. It is their job to bring book proposals to the broader publishing team and convince them to commit to the book that they're championing.

If they succeed, they will work with the author until the final manuscript is delivered and then hand over to the editor for the production of the book to begin.

Editor

An editor is charged with the task of fine-tuning and polishing the manuscript, enhancing the structure and flow of the work, ensuring that any facts are correct, identifying any potential legal problems and sorting out grammatical issues, while all the time respecting the author's voice. Editors have done their job successfully when they leave no obvious trace of their work.

Much of the hands-on editing work in Australia is done by skilled freelance editors, commissioned by the publisher and selected for their experience in a particular genre.

Proofreader

Proofreaders are editorially trained, but they don't proofread a book they've edited. Rather, their job is to come in at the end of the editorial process and read the final manuscript objectively, with a keen eye for any typos, lingering grammatical errors or such small problems as repetition of certain words that the editor may have missed. Their role becomes even more important if a considerable amount of editorial work has been done on the manuscript, which increases the likelihood of mistakes slipping through.

Designer

The designer's job varies in complexity depending on the book. For text-only publications in standard formats, they will focus on the cover, where they need to strike a balance between maintaining the conventions that signal a book's genre, while also creating a striking and individual design. A good designer will read at least some of the book so that they are able to portray the essence of the book to the customer. In publishing, 'Never judge a book by its cover' is a misnomer: the cover is the first thing that alights interest in most prospective purchasers. A typesetter usually does the internal layout of text-only titles, following a standard publisher template.

In illustrated books and non-fiction with graphics and tables, the designer will also be responsible for the page-by-page layout, concentrating on visual appeal and clarity, depending on the content.

Production

When the publisher has approved the final files, production takes charge until the books arrive in the warehouse, organising the eBook conversion and the printing of the physical books. Because of their expertise on special papers and finishes, for an illustrated publication, the production people will form part of the creative team that decides the detail of the final book. In text-only publishing, however, their role will be mostly project management and costs.

DEMYSTIFYING THE ACQUISITION PROCESS

If you're a first-time author, particularly without an agent guiding you, what happens between a publisher expressing interest in your work and signing the contract can be a bit of a mystery. The size of the publisher, the level of publisher interest (if there is more than one publisher involved) and the potential of the book all affect this process, but it generally unfolds as follows.

Every publisher will have an acquisition process, usually involving an acquisition meeting where the decision to publish is made. In a small publishing company, this may simply be an informal discussion between the publisher and their salesperson or distributor about the sales potential for your work. For a medium to large publisher, however, the meeting assembles representatives from every area of the company including editorial, design, production, sales, marketing/publicity and finance.

If you've sent only a sample of your work, the publisher will request the full manuscript to read, if it's available. If you have submitted a proposal only, it's likely the publisher will want to discuss the project with you in more detail. If their reading and discussion confirms their interest, the publisher and/or editor will then put together a proposal to circulate ahead of the meeting, along with a sample of the text. It is their role to champion your work and convince everyone around the table that yours is a great book to add to their publishing program.

The proposal will contain the basic details of the book, which you will have supplied in your submission (more on this later), along with:

- How the book will look: format, extent, etc.
- The proposed retail price and first print run
- A title costing that projects the potential revenue and costs of that first print run, and therefore the margin that the publisher would make. This is to demonstrate that the publication is financially viable and to help set the level of advance, if one is to be offered
- Why the team should acquire the book: how it fits into or complements the publisher's existing list
- Relevant comparative titles
- Any aspects that differentiate this particular proposal, such as the author's social media profile, contacts for cover endorsements, media experience, expertise in the genre of the book and so on.

Acquisition meetings can be very robust because every participant has a different perspective. Sales will usually try to talk down the size of the print run, partly because they want a manageable sales target, but also because they know that the publisher will often try to increase the print run to an unrealistic level if the financials aren't looking good. Finance will want to improve the financial return, which means either lowering costs or increasing the retail price or revenue. Production will resist the pressure to reduce the print and production costs. Marketing and publicity will be trying to manage the publisher's expectations about the level of coverage that can be achieved on publication.

Despite these differing views, a consensus is generally reached and, if luck is with you, your publisher will start preparing the formal offer. If the fates have let you down, however, you should still be encouraged by the fact that your work even reached this stage. It is time-consuming for the publisher to prepare a good proposal and equally time-consuming for the team to read the material, so only a small percentage of the very strongest manuscripts or ideas ever reach the acquisition table. Remember, too, that selecting books for publication is ultimately subjective, so it is certainly worth trying other publishers who may well make a different decision.

SHARE OF THE PIE: HOW THE FINANCIALS WORK

Although writing and publishing books is all about creativity and passion, financial return is, of course, critical. Publishers need to make a profit to have a sustainable business that can continue to acquire books; writers need a fair financial return for the time, care and talent they have poured into their work.

We'll look at the broader financial picture first and then show how the revenue is apportioned for an individual title.

The industry financial view

You may know about the 80/20 rule, known as the Pareto Principle, which asserts that 80% of your results will stem from 20% of your activities. If we apply this to the book industry, and think back to the chart in the introduction, this means that 80% of the revenue comes from 20% of the titles that are published. This trend is right, but in the book world the ratio is probably closer to 90/10.

Of course, every publisher would dearly love to publish only those bestselling titles but they lack the crystal ball that would make this possible. Although this issue isn't confined to publishing, there are businesses in which it's easier to predict the demand for different brands or product categories. In publishing, although overall trends can be observed, past performance isn't a good indicator of success for individual titles because every book is different. *The Da Vinci Code* became one of those mega sellers we talked about earlier, but Dan Brown's previous titles had been very modest performers at best and there was no way of predicting that this book would be different.

Many publishers can have runaway titles that far exceed expectations, but luck and great timing play a significant role in such success. The publisher can only do their best to create a balanced list by managing the risk on new titles and doing their utmost to build a strong backlist, to mitigate the losses incurred by the inevitable failures. It's important to remember this as you start to try placing your book: rejection doesn't necessarily mean that your title wasn't good enough. It may have simply arrived at the wrong time, when a similar title hasn't found its place in the market, or the publisher has taken a big hit on a different book entirely and is seeking safer, more tested books or authors to offset that loss.

Who gets what?

We'll explore the costs of making a book later in this guide, but for now, let's look at how and why the revenue from book sales is split. As you know, there are three financial partners in any book: the publisher, the bookseller and the author. In a typical scenario, using the example of a $20 book, this is how the money breaks up:

Title: $20.00 RRP ex GST	**Author**	**Bookseller**	**Publisher**
Basis of share	10% of retail royalty	45% discount	Receives the rest
$ share per unit	$2.00	$9.00	$9.00

On the surface of it, the poor old author is left out in the cold and the publisher and bookseller are getting the lion's share of the money. But appearances can be deceptive.

We have to factor in the costs incurred by the bookseller and the publisher to better understand what they earn as profit per book sold - the following table uses average costs on a 3,000 copy print run, to demonstrate this.

Bookseller costs	$	Publisher costs	$
Price paid for the book	$11.00	Discount given to bookseller	$9.00
Rent 15%	$3.00	Royalty to author	$2.00
Staff 15%	$3.00	Sales & distribution 25% of revenue from bookseller	$2.75
Marketing/ publicity 5%	$1.00	Production, editorial, design etc, based on a 3,000 print run	$3.00
		Marketing/publicity	$0.50
Services (website, database) 5%	$1.00	Print	$2.25
TOTAL COSTS	**$19.00**	**TOTAL**	**$19.50**

Suddenly the picture looks very different: the author receives $2 for each book sold, the bookseller $1 and the publisher 50 cents.

Of course, every book is slightly different, as is the cost structure for each publisher and bookseller. The picture also changes significantly if the book goes on to sell strongly, because the bookseller then saves money on marketing and probably pays less for the book because they are selling more copies and getting a better discount. Once the publisher starts to reprint the book they no longer have any production costs, and their print price improves because their print runs are bigger. This means that unless the royalty percentage increases as unit sales grow, the author continues to earn a fixed amount per book, while the publisher's and, to a lesser extent, the bookseller's, profit increases.

Our example shows that no one makes much money on a first print run of 3000 copies retailing at $20, but its purpose is to demonstrate that, in order to take the risk on new, untested authors and styles of books, the entire industry relies on the revenue and profit generated by the mega books, along with the steady, low-risk backlist titles. It is also worth noting that both booksellers and publishers have high-cost structures that must be covered by the revenue gained from book sales.

PLEASE BUY MY BOOK

The reasons for a book's success or failure can often be identified in hindsight, but when you consider that a book may be acquired years before it is actually published, prediction is very much harder. No publisher ever brings out a book because they think it will fail. At the time of acquisition, the team believes in the book's potential, and they do their utmost to realise that. The sales and marketing teams do their best to convince retailers, and ultimately the customer, that each book has value, particularly for its target market. Let's look at the ways in which publishers work to maximise the sales of their titles.

Sales

As we've seen, most publishers have access to a sales force, which is usually split into two groups:

1. ***Key accounts:*** This is the person or team who

manage/s the stores that place central buying orders, including discount department stores, Dymocks, Collins, QBD, the airport bookstores, and Booksellers Choice and Leading Edge, which are buying groups of independent shops. They focus on high-volume orders of the lead titles for the month, not range.

2. ***Field sales:*** These are the sales representatives who visit every quality independent bookshop in the country, and their focus is as much on range as on large quantities of major titles.

A sales rep will usually have only an hour's appointment to work through a long list of books, so their relationship with the book buyer is critical. The rep must get to know the strengths and interests of the buyer, including the type of books that have sold well for them in the past, so that they can emphasise the most appealing titles for their customers. This requires trust and respect on both sides; many reps build very strong relationships with their buyers.

Their sales presentations will include covers, information sheets setting out all the data associated with the book, the blurb, the author bio and key selling points. The full manuscript or proof of the major new titles will have already been sent to key customers. The books are sold into stores well ahead of the publication date – between two and three months for the field sales team and three and four months for key accounts, although

Christmas title sell-ins get underway as early as June/July.

All booksellers purchase at a discount off the recommended retail price of the book, excluding GST. They will all have a base discount agreed with each publisher for smaller quantity new titles and backlist. This ranges from 40% to 50%, depending on the size of the store. Larger new title orders, however, will attract a slightly higher discount as the publisher wants to encourage the bookseller to buy more copies so that their most important titles will be more prominently displayed in stores. Almost all books are sold on a sale or return basis, which means that the bookseller pays for the stock on invoice, but they may return any unsold copies to the publisher for a full credit, between three and 12 months after the book's release.

What does this mean in terms of the size of initial orders for new books? In very general terms you might expect the following:

- A new, literary novel without major publisher support could start with orders as low as 500 up to 1,500 on release to independent bookshops, with a smattering of orders from the bigger book chain stores.

- That same novel with significant publisher backing would sell into the chains as strongly as the independents and the initial orders could range anywhere from 3,000 copies upwards, depending on the level of marketing support.

- A commercial novel with major marketing and publicity, known as a lead title, could have an initial order starting from 10,000 copies and sometimes significantly more.

Marketing and publicity

The efforts of the sales team are a very important part of the selling process, of course, but the level of marketing and publicity behind a title also plays an important role, not only in the bookseller's buying decision, but also in how many copies are bought by customers. Because all books are sold on a sale or return basis, maximising sales in the three months after release becomes very important, as most books cannot be returned within this window.

In the past, marketing and publicity were two distinctly different things. Marketing, which included media ads and point of sale collateral for bookshops, occupied the paid side of the equation. Publicity was the unpaid promotional work, which covered author tours and appearances, bookshop signings and launches. Since the advent of social media, however, the line between the two has blurred.

In recent years paid advertising in newspapers and magazines has decreased substantially, as those media channels have shrunk in number and reach. The generation of point of sale collateral for bookshops has also diminished: wastage was high and bookshop layouts have changed. Publishers still pay for marketing, particularly for their books to be included in retailer catalogues, but digital channels have become increasingly important because targeting the right audience can be so much more specific. Word of mouth has always been the most powerful generator of book sales and social media makes it much easier to spread the word widely and quickly.

Increasingly publishers are looking to authors to help with this, which is why, when your book is accepted, you will be asked to detail your social media connections and potential audience. This is particularly relevant for genre fiction such as romance and crime, where many authors are already firmly embedded in large social media communities. It can also be critically important in non-fiction, particularly if the book is relying on the author as expert. Such a writer will have a considerably broader knowledge of, and better links to, the core readers than the publisher.

Being able to support your work in this way is extremely helpful but there are still some tried and true marketing and publicity methods that successfully build interest in new releases.

If you're one of the lucky ones who has been paid a higher-than-average advance and your publisher is pitching your book as a lead title, they could well support it in some of the following ways:

- Ensuring that the sales team meets the author before they sell to bookshops. If you're offered this opportunity, grab it with both hands, because if you can get the reps excited about your work, their passion and commitment will drive a lot of sales. You could be asked to do this virtually, in person or by sending a short pre-recorded video.

- Publishers may try to capture bookseller interest by sending them beautifully produced proof copies of your book in advance of publication, writing personalised letters recommending the title and sometimes setting up events where a group of booksellers can hear about the book directly from you, the author. This personal connection with the book and the author can lead booksellers to recommend your book and sell more copies.
- Advance proof copies help to secure attention, so if your publisher asks you to sign those copies or write a letter to the recipients, then roll up your sleeves.

If your book isn't a lead title, as most aren't, there are still steps that you and your publisher can take to give your book the best chance of success:

- Make sure that you have your elevator pitch down pat, so that whenever anyone asks you about your book you can intrigue them in under a minute.
- In consultation with your publisher, take any opportunity to speak at targeted events that will reach either those who are selling your book or those who will want to read it.

- The same holds true for media interviews, guest blog appearances or any other publicity opportunity: the more often your audience hears about your book, the more likely they are to buy it.
- Provide your publisher with as many niche contacts as possible, particularly if you've written a non-fiction book with a very specific target market.

Finally, we need to address the tough topic of book launches. It's perfectly understandable that an author will want to mark the publication of their book with a celebration, but launches suck up publisher time and resources, often for little reward in either sales or media interest.

If you've written a book that draws on a broad and established market and an event is likely to kick off the word of mouth, then a launch may be worthwhile. It can also work very well if either you or the subject matter of your work is incredibly high profile, and the glitterati and media will attend. Independent booksellers often have very active events programs for their loyal customers. If they love your book, they may be willing to host an event in their shop, with minimal catering.

Overall, however, unless your book falls into one of these groups, it may be best not to push your publisher to hold a launch. It's in your interests for them to use their marketing funds as effectively as possible and, more often than not, a launch is hard to justify. There's nothing stopping you, however, from having a personal party to mark the publication. If you have a strong personal connection to your local bookshop, they could be willing to host a small event and sell books, while you take care of the catering costs. Strong sales at a 'friends and family' launch may help you to get on that store's bestseller list, and thereby improve your word-of-mouth coverage. Just don't expect booksellers to respond well to a request for a launch if you don't already have an established relationship.

THE UGLY DUCKLING BECOMES A SWAN: THE PUBLISHING PROCESS

How does your manuscript get transformed into a book that grabs the attention of the reader as soon as they see it?

Editorial

When the publisher has received and accepted the final manuscript, it will be handed over to the editorial team, where the book production process begins.

In smaller publishers, one editor may do everything, but in larger companies the editorial responsibilities can be broken up into three separate areas:

1. The in-house editor who will act as project manager. This person puts together and then manages the publishing schedule and will be your first point of contact

2. The structural editor who will work with you on the big picture, including any significant reworking that is required. In fiction, they will be concerned with

such matters as plot construction, characterisation and pace. In non-fiction, they may want to look at arrangement of material, for example, or amount of detail and clarity of argument

3. The copy-editor who will address the detail of your manuscript: grammar, spelling, repetition, style consistency, sentence structure.

The editing process can be a little overwhelming if you haven't experienced it before. Every word will be examined, and every extraneous detail excised, along with those long descriptive passages that can often impede the plot's momentum, even though you laboured so hard over their creation. It's worth remembering, however, that every author, including the literary luminaries, has an editor, and they almost all thank them fulsomely because they recognise that it is an editor's objectivity and experience that brings the polish and shine to their work.

> *'It was like removing layers of crumpled brown paper from an awkwardly shaped parcel and revealing the attractive present which it contained.'*
>
> Diana Athill, editor

Editing can also take time, depending on the number of changes that are required, but remember that these are not unilateral. You will be given the opportunity to accept the ones with which you agree and comment on the ones that you dispute. Just do your best to fight any feelings of defensiveness, sleep on your response rather than replying in knee-jerk sensitivity, try to understand why the editor has made the change and dispute only the suggestions that you genuinely believe to be wrong.

Proofs

Once author and editor have agreed on the final version of the manuscript, the book will be laid out in the format required for the printer and the proofing process begins. Ideally there should only be two rounds of proofing: first pages, where you and the editor note any changes and then the second set of proofs, with those changes taken in by the typesetter, for the very final check. If there have been a lot of changes, however, many publishers will undertake a third round of proofing. When you are at final proof stage, the only changes you should make are typos that have been missed, correcting a crucial factual error or any layout problems that have occurred. This is *not* the time for you to change your mind about the way in which you have described a certain character on page x.

Blurb

Potential purchasers browsing in a bookshop are drawn first to a cover and then, almost invariably, they turn the book over to read the blurb. Yes, the blurb should tell them what the book is about, but its aim is not to summarise the intricacies of the plot or detail the contents. It is there to excite interest and persuade people to buy the book.

Despite its size, however, the blurb can become unexpectedly contentious because many authors think that they should write it since they know their own book best. In fact it is often very difficult for writers to distance themselves sufficiently from the book and to employ the marketing buzzwords that will entice buyers.

The blurb or book description has now become even more important, since it forms part of the book's metadata (more on this later), which helps people find your book more easily when they are conducting an internet search.

If you have a marketing background, then by all means have a go at a blurb, but if not, it's best to write a description of the book that you feel happy with and then send it to the editor, who can use this as a base to which they can add some marketing zing.

Design

The level of design that is needed will depend on the genre of your book:

- Fiction and narrative non-fiction will usually be laid out to one of a set of standard templates developed by the publisher and the design is all about the cover
- Instructional non-fiction needs to provide clarity for the reader: graphs, charts, tables and heading formats that illuminate the text
- Illustrated non-fiction requires page by page design, to allow both the text and the illustrations to shine.

Design will be starting while the editing is under way, with draft covers and internal layouts (where appropriate) being prepared and approved. If you have any images or ideas that you would like the publisher to consider for the cover, then it is wise to put these forward early in the production process, although there is no guarantee that they will be used in the final designs. Most publishers will seek your input on the design shortlist, but the final decision will rest with them.

Production

As soon as the manuscript has been finalised and laid out, the page extent – the length of the book – will be established, and the production team can secure final costings for the printing. Apart from illustrated books where formats differ widely, most text-only books will be produced in the standard portrait (vertical) format for their genre, usually in paperback binding:

A format	181 x 111 mm	Mass market fiction and classics in a second format
B format	198 x 128 mm	The second format of most fiction and non-fiction
B+ format	210 x 135 mm	Most commonly used in text non-fiction, literary fiction
C format	234 x 153 mm	First format for both fiction and narrative non-fiction (same size as a standard hardback novel)

Almost all text-only books are printed in Australia, but illustrated titles are still less cost-effective at local printers and will more likely be sent to Asia for printing. This lengthens the print time from between two and four weeks to three months. This longer turnaround includes more proofing time for colour books, to ensure that the illustrations are being well reproduced, as well as the extended shipping time. EBook files are prepared at the same time as the print file, so that they can be loaded onto all key online platforms when the print book is released onto the market. Publishers are increasingly publishing simultaneously in audiobook format as well.

While the editorial and production teams are hard at work making your book, the sales and marketing teams will be starting to plan for publication. This begins much earlier than you might think because of the lead times required by the buyers of the major retail chains, and to give the publicity team enough time to secure media coverage. Ideally the publisher needs to have the selling and marketing material available at least four months before the book is released, though for major Christmas titles this will become at least six months.

Content is king: Readying your work for publication

Before you embark on trying to get your book published, it is vital to understand that you have an obligation to present your work professionally. To achieve this, you must be aware of some important matters that your publisher will expect you to have taken into account in your work. Even if you decide to self-publish, you will still leave yourself exposed to potential criticism or, at worst, legal action, if you have failed to take these steps.

AUTHOR OBLIGATIONS

1. Copyright and permissions

First of all, it's important that you understand the term of copyright and how you establish your copyright over your own work:

- The legal term of copyright in Australia for literary works is generally the life of the author plus 70 years
- There is no registration system for copyright in Australia. As soon as you commit your work to paper, or save your Word document to your computer, copyright protection is automatic. There are unethical companies purporting to register your copyright for an annual fee, but this is a scam. Copyright is free and automatic. It is nonetheless sensible to ensure that your work always bears the copyright symbol, alongside your name and date: © Jane Smith 2022. This serves as a notice to the world that you are the legal copyright owner.

Copyright is breached if someone reproduces your text or illustrations without your permission, or if you do the same thing with someone else's work. You may have heard of some exceptions to this rule, called fair dealing, but these are very specific and are unlikely to apply to a commercial work.

The fair dealing exceptions cover copying for the purpose of:

- Research or study
- Criticism or review
- Parody or satire
- Reporting news
- Providing legal advice
- Providing access to persons with a disability.

In writing your book you may wish to quote from other copyrighted works or to reproduce photographs/illustrations/images from other works. Bear in mind that copyright will be infringed if you reproduce a 'substantial part' of that work without permission. Although this means you are generally allowed to reproduce a short quote from a long book without seeking permission, it is difficult to determine what constitutes a substantial part, because this is not measured merely quantitatively but also qualitatively. You may decide to use a 250-word quote from an 80,000-word work, but if that quote is a key summary of someone's seminal research, you could be in trouble, despite the fact that the quote is so short.

You can obtain guidance on permissions from the Australian Copyright Council, which provides free legal advice to creators. Unless you've sought advice, it's best practice to err on the side of caution and seek permission from the publisher of the work in question. If you want to use a quote from a song lyric, you should check with the Australasian Performing Rights Association and Australasian Mechanical Copyright Owners Society, known as APRA AMCOS, who may be able to confirm the publisher for you. If you want to quote from a book, most medium to large publishers will include information about the permissions process on their website, including online forms that will request the following information:

- Who you are
- What you want permission for
- Why you want permission
- Your willingness to discuss a licence agreement or fee.

The cost of obtaining this permission varies from free to reasonably significant amounts from cultural institutions, depending on the context, the extent of the quote, the placement of an image (e.g. a cover image compared with a small thumbnail in the text), the print run of your book and the scale of its distribution (e.g. Australia only or worldwide). If you are writing for non-commercial reasons, it is worth making this clear in your request as the publisher may then elect to waive a fee.

Even if you don't have to pay, it is important that you receive written permission for all material used and that you acknowledge that usage in your book. If you want to quote from a work that you know to be out of copyright (i.e. copyright has expired), though you do not need permission, you should still always acknowledge the source of the quote.

Most publishers require the author to obtain permissions and pay for them, although some larger publishers may have the resources to help you with this. If you anticipate using many illustrations or quotes, you can try and cap the costs you will incur in your contract.

Unfortunately, tracking down the right person to grant some of these permissions is not always easy, so you need to allow plenty of time as it can take months. If you have genuinely made every possible attempt to locate the copyright owner to no avail, you then need to assess whether you will take the risk and proceed with a disclaimer in place that expresses your willingness to obtain correct permission if the rightful owner comes forward. Your publisher could help you with this risk assessment based on their experience. The Australian Copyright Council can advise you on your legal risks.

2. Bibliography, footnotes, captions and indexing

These most commonly arise in educational publications, but certain categories of trade non-fiction also require some or all of them. Many publishers will have an in-house style sheet setting out their preferred way of managing these. Even if they don't have a formal guide, it is wise to raise this issue with your publisher at the beginning of your project and agree on the format you will use.

The author is always responsible for captions, footnotes and bibliography, although occasionally the publisher will take on the responsibility of the index. The preparation of the index is a skilled job that is usually best left to someone experienced. Even when it is your obligation, publishers will often be prepared to organise for the index to be done and deduct the charge from your royalties. Given the time it can take for the uninitiated, this option is well worth considering.

3. Integrity of content

Language is subjective and fluid as opinions change about what is acceptable. The way in which women were often portrayed in literature in the 1950s, for instance, would now be considered sexist. You can't, of course, predict the way in which societal attitudes will alter, but you must be aware of, and reflect in your writing, the contemporary sensitivities surrounding gender, sexuality, age, culture, religion and race.

4. Cultural sensitivity

In recent years, concerns about cultural appropriation have been hotly debated in the publishing industry. This guide cannot traverse its complexities in detail, but it is important that you think carefully about the issue before and during the writing of your work. The Cambridge Dictionary defines the term as 'the act of taking or using things from a culture that is not your own, especially without showing that you understand or respect this culture' and it was brought sharply into focus for the Australian book industry by Lionel Shriver's controversial speech on the subject at the Brisbane Writers Festival in 2016.

Detractors are quick to claim that it is political correctness gone mad and that, taken to its extreme, it would mean that an author could write only about their own culture and experiences, which flies in the face of writing about such a diverse nation. These arguments, however, seek to trivialise vital principles of respect, historical context and understanding.

So, if you are in any doubt about your portrayal of anything from a historical context to a character from a culture other than your own, ask for help. Consult people from that culture, discuss the issue with them, ask them to read your material and be prepared to make changes if necessary. Above all, always ask yourself the questions, 'Is this my story to tell?' and 'Why am I writing this?' Depending on your subject matter, you may consider engaging a sensitivity reader. Your publisher can guide you, but nothing replaces early awareness, sensitivity and courtesy.

5. Inclusion of Indigenous cultural content

Indigenous cultural material is owned by Aboriginal and Torres Strait Islander peoples and consultation and consent are required before you use, publish or adapt this material in your work.

If your writing or art will incorporate Indigenous Cultural and Intellectual Property (ICIP), you must have regard to industry protocols. The ASA has on its website an excellent paper by Terri Janke and Company that is available free to members: *More Than Words; Writing, Aboriginal and Torres Strait Islander Culture and Copyright in Australia*. This offers guidance on ICIP best practice for every stage of the writing process, which you should read if you are a writer (or illustrator) who is:

- writing about Aboriginal or Torres Strait Islander peoples' issues
- creating Aboriginal or Torres Strait Islander characters
- incorporating in your work Aboriginal or Torres Strait Islander knowledge, traditional stories, ceremonies, language or song
- retelling stories that contain ICIP
- using Aboriginal or Torres Strait Islander iconography, designs or artwork in your work
- using resources or research materials that contain ICIP or refer to Aboriginal or Torres Strait Islander peoples (e.g. archival materials in a state library)
- collaborating with or collecting information or knowledge from an Aboriginal or Torres Strait Islander knowledge holder or community.

6. Sensitivity readers

A sensitivity reader is a beta reader (someone who will read your manuscript before publication and provide feedback) who has the knowledge, experience, and expertise to assess such areas as stereotypes, offensive language, cultural inaccuracies, misrepresentation of marginal groups, bias or archaic or historically inaccurate assumptions. Sensitivity readers are increasingly being used to read fiction written from a perspective with which the author is not personally familiar (e.g. a white straight male writer writing from the perspective of a queer female). Sensitivity readers are not intended to stifle freedom of expression, but to raise your awareness of any unconscious bias or mistakes, and of how your work may be received.

Your publisher might suggest your work be read by a sensitivity reader or you might decide that you are writing outside your lived experience or professional expertise and need a sensitivity reader to review your work for authenticity and accuracy. Like an editor who points out clichés in your writing, a sensitivity reader ought to challenge you to bring nuance and complexity to your work. Using a sensitivity reader does not, however, guarantee that your book will be free from any public scrutiny, should you choose to write from an unfamiliar perspective.

7. Plagiarism

Plagiarism is defined in the Cambridge Dictionary, very simply, as 'copying someone else's work or ideas'. It has increased in recent years because of the ease with which anyone can research online and by the incorrect, but widely held, belief that if it's on the internet, the content is freely available. This is *not* the case. Although research may have become easier, many plagiarism checkers are also now available, which make it much easier to identify when someone has plagiarised. The moral of this story is, don't copy someone else's work, change a few words and think that you've avoided the problem. You can rewrite information in your own words, but it is still courteous to acknowledge the source of this information in a footnote or a reference at the back of the book.

8. Defamation

Defamation is an altogether more complicated problem, which rears its head whenever you are writing about real situations and real people.

You can defame someone in many ways, including making them look ridiculous, dishonest or incompetent. Even implying this can be problematic. You can also defame companies and organisations with fewer than 10 employees and incur liability if you republish a defamatory story or article.

Many people rely on the fact that you can't defame the dead, but this is a case of a little learning being a dangerous thing. Although this is technically true, if you write something dreadful about a person who is dead, their family could still have legal recourse in certain circumstances. The defence of truth is equally tricky: without robust evidence, truth can prove to be a flexible concept, depending on your perspective.

The safest option, therefore, is not to write anything critical about a real person, even if you think you have disguised them with a name change, unless you are completely confident of your facts. Always err on the side of caution and if you have even the slightest doubt, do not make assumptions. Raise the issue with your publisher, who will have access to expert legal advice if necessary or ask the ASA where you can find such advice if you're publishing your own work. If a lawyer recommends that you make changes and you fail to do so, this will likely result in the termination of your contract with a publisher, or potential legal action if you've self-published. The Arts Law Centre of Australia publishes an information sheet on defamation law.

This may seem like a daunting list, and not every aspect that has been covered will be relevant to you. It is important, however, that you double-check your manuscript against this list before you start submitting to publishers as if they see that your manuscript is likely to cause problems in any of these areas, you have substantially reduced your chances of success.

THE POWER OF ASSESSMENT

You have just one opportunity to submit your work to each publisher and so it must be the very best possible version. Given, however, that you will have been hard at work for months, and often years, on your book, you're not in a good position to judge when that moment has arrived, and nor is your mother, aunt or friend. The best first step you can take is to have your work professionally read by an experienced assessor.

Before that you must ensure that your work lies within industry norms in terms of size. Very few publishers or even assessors, will be willing to embark on a 200,000-word crime novel, particularly from a first-time author.

A guide to average word counts:

Adult fiction	• Flash fiction is anything from 100 to 500 words • A short story ranges between 1,000 and 8,000 words • A novella is between 20,000 and 50,000 words • A novel is typically between 75,000 and 90,000 words • Science fiction and fantasy novels are often longer, in the 90,000–110,000-word range
Adult non-fiction	• Narrative nonfiction, including memoir, is similar to a novel at around 75,000+ words • Self-help titles and some business titles tend to be shorter, between 40,000 and 60,000 words • Major history and biography can be longer, up to 120,000 words
Children's	• Picture books between 400 and 700 words, depending on the target age • Early readers, anywhere up to 3,500 words • Chapter books (8–10 years) vary from 5,000 to 10,000 words • Novels (10+ years), 25,000 words • Young adult (YA) starts at 40,000 words but can be up to 80,000 at the upper end of the age range

If your work lies well outside these guidelines, you need to do everything you can to bring your manuscript down to a more reasonable extent. If you genuinely think that this will ruin the integrity of your work, it would be wise to set out your reasons for this when you send the work to an assessor and be prepared to accept their expert opinion if they beg to differ.

Assessment

A good assessor will provide you with a constructive report, setting out any further work that is needed on your manuscript and providing an objective, knowledgeable opinion on the likelihood of publication. For fiction, this report will include any major flaws in the plot, say, or the characterisation or in the standard of writing. This can be confronting, especially if the assessor considers that your work isn't of a publishable standard and is unlikely to ever be so, but it can save you many months of heartache and rejections. Such a report can also provide you with the opportunity to significantly improve your chances of success by improving your work before you start submitting it to publishers.

As is the case with all publishing services, there are many different businesses offering assessments and they're of a very mixed standard. If you're going to base your next steps as an author on this assessment, the person you choose must possess the right skills and experience. Most assessors have a background as an author or a publisher/ editor but such experience in itself does not necessarily mean that they will be good at this job. They must be able to intelligently critique your manuscript, including your writing style, your storyline, characterisation and dialogue if it's a novel, while also understanding the current market conditions, in order to assess not only if your work is of publishable standard, but also whether it might interest publishers. For instance, there are many examples of publishable work by talented writers that have been consistently rejected by publishers because they would appeal only to a very small, niche market.

You need to find out as much as you can about the assessor:

- Where they've gained their experience
- How recent that experience has been, i.e. are they up-to-date with the current market and trends
- Where they're currently working
- Their areas of speciality
- Personal references or reviews from those who've used their service.

And here are a few tips to help you avoid unskilled or unscrupulous operators:

- *Do not* use an assessment offered by a publishing services business. The chances are high that the assessment is being used as a recruitment tool to get you to sign up and then spend a lot more money on other offerings.

- If the business claims to have considerable experience in publishing but does not detail what it is, you should be cautious. A genuinely experienced assessor will be happy to outline their work history
- If the business claims that they can write you letters of recommendation and introduction to publishers, don't be taken in. No reputable publisher or literary agent would take any notice of a letter supplied in this way.

Some organisations that offer manuscript assessment include the ASA, the Institute of Professional Editors, the Manuscript Appraisal Agency and Writers' Centres.

After the assessment

If your assessment is glowingly positive, with few recommendations for change, then you can pour yourself a well-deserved drink and start to plan your submission to publishers.

If it is less positive, however, suggesting that traditional publication is not a viable option, you should first try to distance yourself from the feeling of personal criticism that you're likely to experience when faced with such detailed feedback. Set the report aside for a little while and let the hurt and indignation abate. Then reread the report as objectively as you possibly can, to establish whether at least some of the assessor's remarks are in fact fair. You will then be in a much better position to decide which of the following options will work best for you:

- Seek a second opinion
- Start to rewrite if the assessor has given you good direction on the areas of weakness, and you believe you can overcome these
- Find and work with a mentor (such as via the ASA's mentorship program)
- Focus on the joy of writing, rather than publication, and join a writers' group or take a workshop to develop your skills
- Go ahead with your submission plans, knowing that the chance of success is low
- Depending on your motivations to publish, consider self-publishing, understanding the associated demands on your time, the costs and the limitations.

Choosing the right publishing path

The following charts set out the main pathways to traditional publication and self publication to help you understand the pros and cons and chart the course most suitable for you.

TRADITIONAL

Corporate	Small – Medium
Hachette, HarperCollins, Macmillan, Penguin Random House and Simon & Schuster (significantly smaller in Australia compared with the US)	Affirm Press, Allen & Unwin, Black Inc, Hardie Grant (Ultimo Press for fiction), Pantera Press, Scribe Publishing and Text Publishing are some of the more significant
Almost always source work through literary agents	Larger companies will use literary agents, but many smaller companies will take unsolicited work
Advantages: Publisher pays all costs and carries the financial risk. Has strong relationships with all bookstores, good distribution, and broad media contacts for publicity. Still pays advances	**Advantages:** Publisher pays all costs and carries the financial risk. Good relationships with independent bookstores in particular. May pay advances but will be small. Can be more collaborative than larger players and likely to nurture an author's career. Good at getting new books away
Challenges: Short attention span because handling so many titles. Marketing support only lasts a short time. Try to secure all rights, regardless of whether or not they plan to try and sell them	**Challenges:** Smaller players will not be able to access mass market stores, which is a major problem for commercial/genre titles. Can also find it more difficult to secure a good position for books in-store
An author's best chance at strong sales	**Particularly strong at driving the sales of less obvious, non-genre books**

SELF-PUBLISHING

Self-Publishing	Hybrid/Custom/Vanity
It's all up to you: You choose your own editor and designer and produce your own books	These companies provide publishing services: they make their money from these services, not from the sale of the books. Some traditional publishers also operate a custom publishing division
Best suited to: genre fiction including romance, science fiction and crime and non-fiction with a defined audience, where the author has already established a strong community on social media	Best suited to authors lacking the contacts, knowledge or confidence to manage the production process themselves. Although the self-funded options through traditional publishers can be more expensive, they are generally reliable and of good quality
Advantages: Author retains: • Control • Rights • Revenue • Profit	**Advantages:** The right operator can be fast, and the process can be very simple. Provides access to all digital platforms. If the company is associated with a traditional publisher, the offer may include distribution
Challenges: Author pays all costs and assumes all risk. Access to market is very difficult because there are few distribution options and discoverability is a major issue	**Challenges:** Author pays all costs and assumes all risks. Many unethical companies operating, with exaggerated claims about their capacity to distribute and market effectively
Only the *very* best win, but they can win very big	**Research essential as there are many poor operators in this category**

As you can see from these charts, there are four major paths to publishing open to you. Choices do give you some control over your own destiny, but too much choice can easily become overwhelming. To avoid unnecessary expense and heartache, let's investigate further, to ensure that you don't make an ill-advised decision out of panic or uncertainty.

Why the growth in self-publishing?

For many years this choice was, at best, an unbalanced one: a well-produced, professionally sold and marketed book versus a poorly designed and produced book with almost no marketing or sales support. This inequality was exacerbated by the term 'vanity publishing', with its connotations of an undeserving work published solely because of the ego and resources of the creator. Although this stigma still lingers in some parts of the industry, much has changed in recent years.

First there is the revolutionary change that has taken place in book production. Sophisticated software is now widely available, as is access to the same skilled freelance designers and editors used by most traditional publishers. This means that the books poorly laid out on a desktop computer, once the only alternative for most authors, should be a thing of the past.

The same transformation has occurred on the print side. Short run printing and print-on-demand used to be extremely expensive and poor quality but now, at least for non-illustrated books, it is possible to print on good quality paper at an affordable cost at a range of local printers. EBooks have widened the market further by providing access to a global market that can purchase any book at the click of a button. The more recent growth in audiobook sales has increased this reach, although access to high-quality audiobook production is only now becoming readily available for the self-published.

These changes have gone a long way towards equalising the two publishing options, tempting more and more authors to abandon the search for a traditional publisher in favour of the perceived freedom and increased income offered by the alternative. There is, however, still one major stumbling block on the self-publishing route: discoverability. How do potential customers not only know that your book has been published, but also where they can buy it?

As the barriers to self-publishing have lowered, increasing numbers of people have set their sights on becoming published authors, which has inevitably led to an ever more crowded online marketplace. Even though it is a straightforward process to make your eBook available on all the major global retail platforms, how do people find your book among the millions of available titles?

The situation with print books is no better, because very few distributors are willing to sell single titles into bricks and mortar bookshops. And there is the same problem of how you tell your potential buyers that your book is available.

Keys to self-publishing success

Despite these challenges, many thousands of authors are self-publishing their work every year and although it is difficult to obtain accurate data, it is reasonable to assume that the sales pattern resembles that of traditional publishing: a very small number of titles generating a significant proportion of the overall revenue. It is apparent, however, that certain categories of writer have greater chances of self-publishing success:

- Genre fiction writers, particularly in romance, crime and science fiction, where the sales of eBooks are high, who have built substantial and highly supportive online communities
- Non-fiction writers with an established social media community and following in their area of expertise
- Previously published authors with an established online presence and high numbers of loyal readers.

If you and your work fall into one of these categories, and you have already built a large online profile, then self-publishing can be a realistic option to investigate. But *do not rush*. Do your research carefully and talk to as many authors as possible who have managed their own publications. They will usually be very open to sharing their mistakes and triumphs. Above all, be realistic about your own skills. If, for instance, you have little experience in digital marketing and social media, you need to consider how you're going to manage this side of the publication process. You must also be realistic about the time commitment required to support and market your book both in the lead-up to publication and after it has been published.

If you've considered all the options and your mind is made up, feel free to skip to Part III, which covers the self-publishing path in greater detail.

But if you want to self-publish because you believe you'll make more money, or you'd prefer to control your own destiny, proceed with caution. If your work doesn't fall into any of those three categories, and your manuscript assessment is positive, then the traditional publishing path is likely to be a more suitable option.

PART 2

PART 2

Traditional publishing

One of the first decisions you face when you set off on the traditional publishing path, is whether you're going to try to find a literary agent.

Literary Agents

A literary agent's primary role is to find a publisher for the work of the authors that they represent and then help those authors to manage and build their career. Ideally, an agent will bring the following skills and experience:

- Knowledge of the local publishing network, along with the ability to target the right company, and the right editor/publisher within that company, for your work
- Experience in writing compelling submissions

- A comprehensive understanding of publishing contracts
- Excellent negotiation skills
- A thorough working knowledge of the publishing process
- A range of international contacts to help secure interest from overseas publishers
- The resources and experience to manage the financial and business aspects of your career, including royalty payments, scrutiny of royalty statements and the negotiation and management of sub-licences
- The experience to help you make the right choices and work with you to develop a sustainable career.

HOW DO YOU DECIDE IF YOU NEED AN AGENT?

Writing talent doesn't automatically bring with it the skills to navigate the publishing landscape, negotiate complicated agreements and make decisions that may affect your career for many years to come. A good agent can free you up to focus on your creative work. In some circumstances, however, the need for an agent may be less pressing, for example, if:

- You have a proven track record in publishing
- You have strong personal contacts within the industry

- You have acquired experience in understanding and negotiating contracts
- You know how to work effectively with a publisher
- Your work is in a niche area in which the agent is unlikely to have as much experience as you do.

If you fall into any of these categories, you may know which publishers suit your work best and have direct access to those people, so an agent may be unnecessary.

If, however, you're a first-time or inexperienced author, then it can be more difficult to reach a publisher without the help of an agent. Not only are the slush piles (manuscripts sent in by authors on spec) huge, but also many of the larger publishers primarily work through agents and discourage or avoid direct submission. They do this to avoid the sheer volume of unsolicited manuscripts they would otherwise receive.

We'll look at the ways in which you can secure an agent, but if you're unsuccessful, don't despair: we'll also cover the ways in which you can improve your chances of success by yourself.

How do you find an agent?

This isn't easy. There are large numbers of writers trying to get their work published, but only a very limited number of literary agents. This means that they can afford to be very selective and many close their lists to new writers.

This is disheartening, especially for first-time authors, but there are some steps you can take to overcome this problem. Publishing is pre-eminently a relationship business. Many agency staff have worked in the industry for a long time and have built up a network of contacts whose opinions they trust. Good research and good referrals can, therefore, help you to gain access.

The place to start is the website of the Australian Literary Agents Association (ALAA), where you will find a list of literary agents with their contact details so that you can access their websites. This is helpful because you can then see the range of authors they represent, find out if they are accepting new submissions and, if so, in what format. The list is not comprehensive, however, since the association admits only full-time agents as members, whereas many agents supplement their income with other freelance work.

Further ways to research:

- Look at the ASA's listing of literary agents, available on their website
- Check out individual author websites and blogs as many will mention their agent
- When reading books in your genre, take note of the agents being thanked in the acknowledgments
- Join author blog sites/Facebook groups etc. Authors are often very generous about sharing information
- Subscribe to relevant industry newsletters such as *News from the ASA* and *Books+Publishing*.

As you begin to build your list, make sure that you focus on the types of authors and genre each agent represents. Because finding an agent is difficult, there's a temptation to adopt the scattergun approach, but you're only wasting your time and theirs by sending your children's picture book to an agent specialising in adult non-fiction. It is also very important to take careful note of an agent's submission requirements and fulfil those to the letter. If they ask for 10 pages, then that's what you send.

A referral from a respected industry or author contact is another excellent way to approach an agent, although once again, not easy if you're a first-time author. There are, however, ways you can try to overcome this:

- ASA's Literary Speed Dating (LSD) event, where you have an opportunity to pitch your work directly to Australian agents and publishers. If you're not confident about this prospect, keep an eye out for Pitch Perfect, the pitching training session that is held a few weeks before each LSD event
- Join any group that is relevant to you and your writing, or find a mentor for your work, as these are potential sources of suitable referees
- Look for any opportunity to attend events where agents will be present in a professional capacity, e.g. writers' festivals and other industry events
- Enter any relevant competitions or awards: it's part of an agent's job to watch out for new talent appearing on shortlists.

It is, however, critical to exercise good judgement and behave respectfully. A social gathering is *not* the place or time to monopolise an agent with a 10-minute monologue about your work. It's also discourteous to ask another writer for a referral to their agent unless they know you and your work well and have already expressed an interest in helping you. The publishing industry can be very generous, but it's a tight-knit community, and it doesn't take long for word to spread if you allow your enthusiasm to run away from you.

HOW THE AUTHOR/AGENT RELATIONSHIP WORKS

A warning, to begin with. As with any profession, a small number of people have set up as agents because they see an opportunity to make money by exploiting the many authors desperate for representation. It is imperative that you check out any prospective agent's background and, if possible, talk to some of their authors before you make any commitment. Successful agents rely on their publishing contacts and connections, so step away if your research reveals that an agent has little or no industry experience. If the agent asks for money up-front, either by way of a reader's fee or a 'down payment' of any kind, this is also reason for concern. Such arrangements are not standard industry practice. An agent gets paid by way of a percentage of the advance and royalties when they successfully place a book with a publisher.

If you have been able to secure an agent's interest, you

must start your relationship by signing an agreement that sets out:

- The books the agent will represent: specify in an attached title listing
- The territories and rights that you have granted them: again, specify a list
- The financial arrangement: typically, an agent takes 15% commission on total revenue earned on the titles/rights that you have granted
- Termination: usually a month's notice but can be up to three.

The ASA has a model Literary Agents Agreement on its website which shows you what to expect. Territories and rights will be discussed in more detail in the section dealing with the publishing contract, but if you consider that your book has international potential, you may want to grant those rights to your agent. That can be appropriate, but make sure that you discuss this before you sign an agreement.

Some agents are very well positioned to secure overseas deals. They may attend international book fairs or have done so in the past, so they have a healthy contacts list, or they may work through sub-agents. These are agents based in the different markets around the world, who work to license your rights in their territory, on behalf of your agent. Such sales incur an additional commission, often between 2.5% and 5%.

If you have no global contacts and are uncertain about the strength of your agent's connections, there are ways to manage this, including granting the rights for a fixed period of time or withholding them from the agent agreement and granting them directly to your publisher.

It's equally important that you understand how an agent agreement works:

- The publisher pays all your royalty and rights income to your agent, who deducts their commission and then pays the balance to you as the author. They should do this as quickly as possible, ideally within 10 days of receiving the money
- The agent can also deduct expenses such as postage and international phone calls but it's best that these expenses are specified in the contract
- Although it's usually quite straightforward to terminate your agency agreement (by giving one to three months' written notice), note that the agent receives what are called *residuals,* based on the duration of the publishing agreements they negotiated on your behalf, which is often for life of copyright. This means that the agent continues to receive their commission on your earnings from *every* deal they made while your agency agreement was in place, even after the agency agreement is terminated. They also receive income for any deal that is being negotiated when the termination is issued

- So, when you negotiate your agreement with your agent, it is worthwhile trying to negotiate that this residual income is limited to a period of time, ideally between seven and 10 years following termination, after which time the agent ceases to have any financial interest in your work.

Don't forget that you can submit a literary agent's contract for review by Author's Legal, the low-cost legal service offered to ASA members.

A final word of advice. Once you've signed a deal with your publisher, your agent takes a back seat while the book is being produced, stepping in only if there's a dispute or problem. As you start to build strong relationships with your publishing team it can be very tempting to believe that you no longer need an agent, especially when you're attempting to earn a living wage as a writer. Of course, if your agent isn't doing their job, then you have every right to discuss this with them and possibly resort to termination, but it can be very short-sighted to make this decision for financial reasons alone. Staff at publishing companies change very quickly and the relationships that you have built there could easily disappear overnight. Your agent is the one constant who always has your back, who can see you through all the ups and downs of your writing life. Deciding to save money when times are good can cause big problems further on in your career.

Going solo (without an agent)

If you haven't been able to find an agent, all is not lost, but you'll need to set about finding the right publisher for your work. In many ways this is a similar process to finding the right literary agent, but even more important.

This will sound counter-intuitive, but it's essential to curb your enthusiasm. It is, of course, a powerful motivator, but if you don't keep it in check, it can lead you to make some fundamental mistakes. You need to be very considered and targeted as you prepare your publisher prospects list.

There's no rush. If you've spent the past three years writing your book and it's finally finished, you're understandably eager to see it published as quickly as possible, but this desire has nothing to do with publishers and their timelines. If you sacrifice thoroughness for speed and simply prepare a standard submission that you send to every publisher you can think of, your chances of success are almost non-existent.

Publishers aren't all the same. They have different areas of interest and expertise, and it's your job to research these and find the best match for your work. Sending a mass market fiction title to a literary publisher won't get you anywhere. These are the best ways of drawing up your own shortlist of prospective publishers:

- Look at your own bookshelves: it's likely that you read in your areas of writing interest, and you may start to see a pattern in the publishers you have unintentionally been supporting

- Roam your local bookshop and note which publishers are dominant in your category. Talk to your local bookseller, who will have great insights into which publishers are best in your category (but not at lunchtime, with no appointment!)
- Check out the lists of major award winners in your genre, which will highlight publishers who specialise in that area
- Read reviews
- Talk to authors in your genre.

Once you've assembled a list of potential publishers, try placing them in order of importance, taking into account factors such as:

- Personal contact, if you have one
- Number of books in your genre that are on their list
- Whether they have a specialist imprint devoted to your subject matter
- Reputation
- The quality of their production
- The degree of marketing and publicity support they give to their authors.

When you're happy with your targeted and prioritised list, check each of the publisher's submission requirements carefully and put together your first two or three submissions. One of the most frequently asked questions at this point is whether you can submit your work to more than one publisher at the same time.

Publishers can be sensitive about multiple submissions, as each likes to feel that they have the inside running, but it can take many months to work through a slush pile. If you wait to hear back from each publisher before you send your work to your next prospect, it could take you years to get through your list. This still doesn't mean that you should approach as many publishers as you can think of, but sending your proposal simultaneously to your best three or four is acceptable.

Some publishers will request that you advise them if you've submitted to other publishers. If you have, then you should say so. If they don't specifically ask, it's your decision whether to mention this. You don't have to tell them, although there's no reason to withhold this information.

If one of those publishers expresses interest in your work, however, you should let them know, if you haven't already, that your work has gone to other selected publishers. Then follow up with the other publishers by sending a polite email saying that there's interest in your work, and you would be grateful if they could let you know if they want to take your submission any further. Publishing is a competitive business: knowing that your work is being assessed by one of their competitors will likely ensure that your work miraculously rises to the top of their slush piles.

Preparing a winning submission

Every publisher will specify their own requirements for submissions, and it is vital to observe these, but almost every submission process has some basic pieces of information and rules in common. You should be able to readily adapt the following to conform with almost any individual publisher permutation.

PURPOSE OF A SUBMISSION

A submission isn't designed to provide a detailed outline of every twist and turn in your ingenious plot. Its purpose is to interest the publisher in your work and present a sound business case for publication. This may seem obvious, but it is amazing how many authors fail to grasp what's required. Writing is a creative and artistic activity, but a publisher is running a commercial business and their role is to select books that appeal to enough readers to make them financially viable for both author and publisher. Keep this at the forefront of your mind throughout the preparation of your submission. Who will buy my book and why will they buy it?

First, though, let's take a minute to examine what a publisher looks for in an author – apart from a readable manuscript of publishable standard which they believe has the potential to sell well.

- ***Your platform:*** As the number of books being published continues to grow, discoverability becomes increasingly difficult, even for a well-established publisher. As a result, an author's ability to support their book has taken on a new significance. Depending on the genre, this can include blogs, social media, workshops, events and everything in between.

- ***Your credibility:*** This is where your track record, either as a published author or as an expert in your field, will be important.

- ***Your future publishing potential:*** It takes time, effort and resources for a publisher to market a book effectively and they'll be much keener to make this level of commitment if they know that you have the interest and capability to write more books. Obviously, this is less important if they see significant sales potential in your current work.

- ***Sticking to your genre:*** Ideally, a publisher would prefer you to continue writing in the same genre because this makes it easier to build you as a brand.

Not all these factors will be relevant to your work, but it is worthwhile to use them as a point of reference when you are compiling your submission.

CONTENTS OF A SUBMISSION

Let's begin by ensuring that you have all the base data that you're likely to need:

- Your contact details
- The title of your book
- Whether it's fiction (+ genre), non-fiction (+ category), children's (+ age group)
- The word count
- Whether the manuscript is finished or a time frame to complete it.

You can then turn your attention to the competitive analysis. This will include:

- The target market for your work. Who will buy it?
- The size and accessibility of that market
- Comparative titles
- Where and why your book fits the publisher's list.

Then it's on to the content. Different publishers will have different requirements here, but it is wise to prepare the following, and be ready to edit to meet different word count requirements:

- A one-sentence hook, similar to a shout line or subtitle on a book. This could be the first sentence in your cover letter, or the lead-in to your synopsis, but wherever you use it, its purpose is to attract the attention of the recipient and entice them to read on

- A three- to four-sentence overview of the book
- The synopsis, which can range from 200 to 500 words. Regardless of the length, it is critical that you identify the key features of the plot, the major characters and the overall arc of the story. Make sure you show how the plot is resolved. The suspense of the ending is for the readers, not the acquiring publisher
- An excerpt of your book, which can be anything from a set number of words or pages, up to the complete manuscript. Choose this carefully, to show your writing in the brightest light.

If you've written an adult novel, the content section of your submission, especially the synopsis, must reflect the book's style and tone, whether it's serious or more humorous and playful. You also need to put time and thought into the comparison titles you provide, as this will demonstrate your level of insight about your own work.

If your work is non-fiction, then you must prepare a chapter outline with a sentence explaining each chapter. Your author bio is vital too, because this establishes your credentials to write on your chosen subject. Indeed, many publishers will ask you why you're the right person to write this book and you need to be able to prove that you are. If your work is illustrated, you should also provide a short section detailing where this material is coming from, and, ideally, who owns the copyright.

If you are a children's writer, the same rules for fiction and non-fiction apply, but it's also important to show that you understand the language level and complexity of the age group for which you're writing. There is additional information for illustrators beginning on page 90.

Finally, there will be a section about you as the author. Again, this will be restricted in length so you must shape your CV so that it connects to your book. Publishing history is critical if you're not a first-time writer, as are any awards you may have received, including those for unpublished works. If you've written previous books, don't lie about the sales. Almost every publisher has access to BookScan data which gives them accurate data on the entire sales of any book in the Australian market.

THE MUST DOS

Attention to detail

An astonishing number of authors send off a submission to a publisher without taking the time to edit or proofread it. Sometimes even the name of the publishing company is incorrect. This sort of carelessness, along with poor grammar and spelling mistakes, is unacceptable. Indeed, it would be hard to think of an easier way for a publisher to reject your proposal. Be careful. Get a professional editor to check the main sections of your submission and read over your cover letter thoroughly. If you haven't bothered to get your submission up to standard, there's no way that a publisher is going to consider investing thousands of dollars in producing your book.

Adhere to submission requirements

Every publisher's website will itemise exactly *what* they want to receive in a submission and *when* they want to receive it. You must observe these instructions to the letter. Of course, it's annoying to prepare a different submission for each publisher, but it's essential if your work is to have any chance of being considered. Make sure, too, that you pay careful attention to the timing of your submission. Some publishers are willing to accept work at any time, but many others specify a particular day or window when they will open their portal for unsolicited proposals. Just remember that the slush pile is large and the person in charge of vetting the submissions is looking for easy ways to reduce it. Submissions that fail to conform to the clearly specified requirements or timing are the first to go on the reject pile, without anyone having read a word.

Personalisation

Wherever you can, personalise your submission to a particular publisher, and, in the case of the large publishers, ideally target your work to a specific imprint or the person running it. Every imprint will have its own flavour, reflecting the taste of the person acquiring the list, so if you can compare your work to books with which the publisher has had past success, you improve the chances of your work being read. A well-considered cover letter can also help your submission stand out from the crowd. Keep your tone professional and don't feign familiarity with the person to whom you're writing, if you've never had any personal contact.

Take your time

Unless your book is topical or there is some other major reason for haste, there is no pressing need to submit it immediately. If you get this step wrong, the publisher won't even read your manuscript, so you need to treat your proposal with the same level of care that you gave to your work. Revise and reread, revise and reread so that every word of the meagre allowance given by the publisher really counts. You only get one opportunity to make a first impression, so don't blow it because of a self-imposed sense of urgency.

THE DON'TS

Resist the temptation to include any of the following, especially in the opening sentences of your letter. Not only will they not help, but you also run the risk of your submission being summarily dismissed:

- That you have spent x number of years writing your book: Your problem
- That becoming a published author is your dream: Only you care
- That you are a great writer, and they will be sorry if they miss out: Red Flag
- That your work is similar to *Harry Potter* (or any other mega seller): Read no further
- That your best friend/mother thinks you are a genius: Utterly irrelevant.

Resources

There are many resources available on the preparation of a good submission, but these are three of the most reputable and useful: the ASA's regular course, Pitch Perfect, which, as mentioned earlier, focuses on the most effective way to pitch your work to a publisher, both in writing and in person; Jane Friedman is an experienced publishing professional with a website and blog that contains some excellent resources for writers; Reedsy is another publishing blog with helpful information on the topic.

CHILDREN'S BOOKS AUTHORS AND ILLUSTRATORS

Although this general advice on submissions is relevant to children's authors and illustrators there are some specific areas that need to be addressed in children's submissions.

Before we begin, a couple of general pieces of advice if you're thinking of turning your hand to children's books. Some aspiring authors look at the low word counts in children's books and conclude that it must be both quick and easy to dash one off without too much effort. They couldn't be more wrong. There is considerable skill involved in writing for children.

The vocabulary must be pitched correctly for the target age group, as must the context, so that the books challenge, entertain and stimulate the child, while retaining their interest. When there are not many words involved, every one counts. And then there's the rhythm, which is critically important in books that will be read aloud. Indeed, the only way to road test the text for a children's book is to read your work aloud and ask others to do the same for you. This will help you to identify where the flow may be faltering.

International sales in children's picture books can be more difficult, for two reasons. The first is that different markets can have very different expectations of what is age appropriate and what constitutes diversity. The second is that translation into other languages can be challenging, because word length can vary widely. For example, a Spanish text could be as much as 30% longer than the English equivalent, which can create problems with book design. Such challenges are exacerbated if the text is in rhyme.

Children's books are, of course, frequently sold internationally, but it's usually best to write for your primary market in Australia first. If your book is a success in its own country, an overseas publisher will feel happier about any additional costs involved in publishing your work for their market.

Illustrated books: authors

A picture book is led by the text. In other words, the publisher almost always finds the author first, and then selects the illustrator they believe will best complement what has been written. High-profile authors will often have an established relationship with an illustrator or have a great deal of influence over the selection. For newer or first-time authors, the publisher will expect to commission the illustrator. The same holds true for books aimed at young readers which include black and white illustration.

Because, in a good picture book, both the words and the illustrations tell the story, it would be understandable to assume that the author and illustrator collaborate closely, but this is not always the case. The publisher not only commissions the illustrator but also oversees the book's design. Indeed, industry protocol is that the author should not annotate the manuscript for the illustrator, unless there is some object or clue that is not obvious in the text but should be illustrated.

The publisher will work separately with the author to edit the text.

Children's books: illustrators

So how do publishers go about selecting an illustrator? Because children's publishers often have considerable experience and many contacts, when they discover a text they love, they may well have a specific illustrator in mind. If this isn't the case, they can use other avenues, including:

- Their own list of illustrators with whom they have worked before or whose portfolios that they have kept on file
- Illustrator websites that curate content from many different artists, such as the ASA's Style File
- Illustrator showcases, conferences and book fairs
- Illustration agencies and literary agencies that represent illustrators

- An illustrator's work they may have seen in other books or elsewhere
- Author recommendation.

Once the illustrator has been commissioned, the publisher will work with the author to edit the text and then give the illustrator a full design brief. Many illustrators will both provide the artwork and design the layout of the book, under the direction of the publisher (and, accordingly, should be paid an additional design fee). If an illustrator is new to the book industry, a book designer will complete the layout.

Given that the story comes first, it is rare for the illustrator (unless author and illustrator are one and the same person), to initiate a picture book project, so how do illustrators, particularly those new to publishing, attract the attention of publishers?

The first step is to prepare the best possible portfolio of your work, something that will stand out from the crowd and remain memorable.

- Include only your very strongest work
- Demonstrate your range, but don't overdo it: 10–15 pieces should be sufficient. A 20-page maximum is the industry standard
- Although most work will be in colour, it's always wise to include a few black and white examples as well
- Showcase the mediums that you use most frequently and that you can afford to do. If your technique takes

significant amounts of time, it may not be possible for a publisher to justify it financially

- Particularly if picture books are your area of interest, make sure that you include both children and animals and demonstrate a variety of movement and expression. Characterisation is key: publishers like to see how consistently you can maintain characters in different scenes.

Some first-time illustrators take the step of also making a dummy or 'flatplan' of a picture book to show that they understand layout and design. This certainly isn't essential and can be very time-consuming. If you do decide on this, you can use some of your own text or illustrate a previously written book, with a couple of complete colour works or spreads and then roughs for the rest of the book. Always remember that you're telling a story through your artwork.

Once you've assembled your portfolio, you're ready to start distributing it. Some children's publishers will outline a process for the submission of portfolios on their website, but if they haven't done this, then the process becomes the same as outlined earlier. Research the publishers you think best fit your work, take the time to seek out their name and direct contact details and then send them a polite email offering to come in and show your original portfolio or mention your willingness to send through a higher resolution file if that would be helpful. Attach your portfolio at a size that will be easy for the viewer to manage at the other end.

At the same time, place your portfolio on the websites that the publishers use when searching for new talent. Some of these will require you to become a member of the relevant organisation, but most of those groups also offer resources and advice that can be very useful, so it is certainly worth doing.

Contractual issues and self-publishing illustrated children's books will be covered in the appropriate sections later in this guide.

Resources

The ASA has excellent children's book specialists on its mentor register, so if you would like to work up your text or portfolio with an expert this is a great place to start.

The ASA also runs a curated portfolio website, The ASA Style File, for illustrator members where you can submit your portfolios.

The SCWBI (Society of Children's Book Writers and Illustrators) has a membership partnership offer with the ASA, and not only has a showcase for illustrators, but also a very useful handbook that is available to all members.

THE WAITING GAME

This is one of the hardest steps in the publishing process, and sometimes the longest. Some publishers include their turnaround time in their submission guidelines, but on average expect to wait at least three months, so it's wise to always make a diary note of when you submitted to each publisher and when you might expect to have an answer.

Although this waiting can seem interminable, resist the urge to follow up with the publisher until their nominated time has elapsed. Early contact won't speed up the process and it can be seen as an annoyance, which won't help your chances. If you've heard nothing by the end of the period, then a courteous phone call or email requesting a new assessment date is certainly acceptable – but only if the publisher has made it clear that they will eventually respond. Some publishers will contact you only if they have further interest in your work, so if you've had no response in the designated time, you'll have to face the fact that they're not interested in your submission.

Rejection

Rejection is a tough word, and even though there's hardly a writer on the planet who hasn't had to deal with it, often many times over, it still hurts, and it still feels personal. This sense of failure is not helped by the fact that most rejection letters don't tell you why your work isn't wanted, but probably merely use a stock phrase like 'Your work doesn't fit the profile of our list'. Publishers do this because they're swamped with manuscripts and can't risk opening a dialogue with every author they reject. This is understandable, but of no help to you.

Publishers are spoilt for choice, but they don't reject to be unkind or because they don't care. They turn down work for a variety of reasons, usually because the writing isn't of a publishable standard. But good books can be, and sometimes are, rejected, thanks to other factors:

- The potential market may be considered too small to make a print run viable and justify the level of investment
- The genre may be problematic for the publisher
- They may consider that you don't have a sufficiently strong network/marketing background or capability
- Your work may be good, but not stand out sufficiently to have a strong chance of success.
- Your work just doesn't appeal to the taste of the editor who assessed it.

Many writers' blogs and websites deal with rejection, and almost every one of them will exhort you to keep going or self-publish, but is this always the answer or is there a time when you should admit defeat?

If you've had a rejection letter that does set out the reasons for that rejection and suggests ways that you could potentially remedy the problems, you should take this as a positive sign. If a publisher has taken the time to provide reasons for the rejection, there's some hope that they could become interested if the troublesome areas were addressed.

Read the critique carefully and if you understand and agree with the feedback and believe you can solve the problems, then write and thank the publisher for their constructive response, confirm that you're rewriting along the lines they have suggested and propose that you resubmit to them directly when you've finished. Then get to work.

If you've received a standard rejection without explanation, but your work is genuinely endorsed and supported by knowledgeable and experienced industry advisers, such as professional assessors and mentors, then try to objectively reassess your submission and press on. Many successful authors list perseverance as one of the keys to their success.

But if you started submitting without a positive assessment or any other ringing endorsements, your work may simply not be publishable. This is hard to take, and you may decide to carry on and self-publish anyway, but don't forget that the readers of self-published books are the same readers who buy traditionally published books, and they're not easily fooled. Saving your money and writing for pleasure, or for your family, or changing to a different genre and trying again, are all worth considering.

Success: an offer of publication

The other response to a submission is, of course, an expression of interest and ultimately an offer to publish your work. The magic wand has been waved and your life as a successful, wealthy, respected author unfolds before you as you reach for your pen to sign the offer. Stop, though, and take your time. If you have an agent, they will negotiate with the publisher and guide you through the contractual process, but if you don't have an agent, there are steps that you must work through to at least ensure that you're aware of any potential issues before you sign.

Any strong business partnership depends on a good working relationship between the two primary parties and the publisher/author relationship is no exception: it relies on mutual respect, professionalism and a shared goal. It's extremely important to do your homework and to be comfortable with the relationship you're entering into. You and the publisher could potentially work together for years and if alarm bells are ringing early on, it's likely that a poor situation will continue to deteriorate as the stress of deadlines kicks in. Only you can tell how serious your reservations may be, so trust your instincts. A badly published book that doesn't sell won't help you to build your writing career.

The publisher, too, wants a good relationship with you in order to maximise the sales potential of your work. But don't pretend to have certain skills or experience because you know that's what the publisher wants to hear. You won't be able to fake it forever and you'll only sour your relationship when it becomes clear that you don't know your Instagram from your TikTok. Own up to gaps if they exist but demonstrate your willingness to learn and take direction.

The luxury of choice

Understanding the dynamics of the publisher/author relationship becomes even more important if you're in the fortunate position of having several publishers interested in your work. Of course, the financial side of an offer is important, but the size of the advance often becomes the sole focus of the deliberations, and this can be a mistake. Although a healthy advance does signal the level of commitment that the publisher is making, in the end it's only an early payment of royalties earned. It's just as important to compare some of the attributes discussed earlier in this section:

- Is there one publisher who seems to place a higher value on production quality?
- What is each publisher's track record in marketing and supporting their books?
- Do the titles from one publisher seem to have a higher profile in the market?
- What do their authors say about them?
- The intangibles: Do you like the people you'll be working with? Do you trust their judgement? Do you feel comfortable with their plans for your book?

Your decision can become particularly difficult if the interested publishers occupy very different areas of the publishing spectrum, e.g. a large corporate versus a smaller independent business. All the above factors will play into your decision, but a summary of the pluses and minuses of each option may also be helpful.

Refer to the tables below to see the pros and cons of publishing with a large corporate publisher as opposed to publishing with a smaller independent one.

Corporate pluses	Corporate minuses
Resources: own sales force, strong market share, publicity/marketing, editorial and production capacity and budget	Very large lists so the major books get the most resources
Strong market reach, especially large accounts	Short window in terms of promotion (2–4 weeks), before the team has to move on to the next round of new titles
Strong media relationships	May be less likely to develop an author if initial sales don't meet expectation
Prestige	

Indie pluses	Indie minuses
Experience at generating strong word of mouth	Fewer resources and, depending on the size of the business, may not have such a direct relationship with the sales team
Excellent indie bookshop relationships in particular, which generate word of mouth	Financial constraints may inhibit ability to negotiate catalogue placements and large central orders which all come at a cost to the publisher
May be more likely to work with an author for the long term	Don't enjoy the same economies of scale as larger players
Smaller lists allow greater individual title focus	

In the end, there's no right or wrong answer. All you can do is think carefully about the audience for your book, so that you can assess which publisher is most likely to be able to reach and nurture that market. But above all, trust your gut. Size isn't everything and if you trust and like the publisher, and they have a proven track record, your decision is made.

The role of the publisher

Before we move on to the negotiation and signing of the all-important author contract, let's clarify the roles and responsibilities of the publisher.

The publisher is responsible for the process, decisions and costs of turning your manuscript into a finished book, in print, digital or audio formats. These responsibilities include three major areas:

Production: including editorial, proofing, design and layout and printing or formatting into eBooks and/or producing as an audiobook. Although most publishers will consult with the author and genuinely try to take their opinions into account, they make the ultimate decisions as they pay all the costs.

Sales and marketing: includes the costs and management of the sales team that sells all new titles to the booksellers, along with the marketing and publicity support that is designed to boost sell-through in stores.

Distribution: the operational side of publishing, including the invoicing of bookseller orders and the physical receipt of stock from printers and its distribution to stores.

The author contract demystified

Before we move on to the contract itself, there are a couple of general warnings to bear in mind.

Warning 1: Letter of offer

Increasingly publishers are beginning the sign-up process by sending a letter that sets out the key terms of the agreement. These include delivery date, planned publication date, advance, royalty rate, the term of the agreement and grant of rights. The author will then be asked to sign this letter before the full contract has been issued.

The problem with this approach is that you're agreeing to something without having all the facts. The commercial terms might be acceptable to you, but when you receive the contract, you could find problematic clauses such as a high discount trigger set at a low 50% discount, no termination clause or an onerous non-compete, all of which are explained in more detail in the contracts section below. Also, if you're seeking advice on a contract, your lawyer or agent will want to see the full contract rather than go through two rounds of negotiation.

If the publisher does send you such a letter, it's best to politely respond by asking for a copy of their standard agreement to consider alongside their offer. Even if they haven't yet customised the contract for your specific book, it will give you details on the clauses that could be problematic and which you can then flag with the publisher upfront. If you choose to sign the 'deal terms' outlined in the letter, a prudent approach is to make very clear that your agreement is subject to seeing and agreeing to the entire contract.

Warning 2: Seek advice before signing

The second important warning is that, regardless of your excitement at finally being offered a publishing deal, it's absolutely critical that you do *not* sign that agreement without reading it very thoroughly and seeking professional advice. If the offer is from a mainstream traditional publisher, the chances are high that their contract will largely conform to industry standards, but it's worth remembering that any legal agreement is going to favour the party that drew it up in the first place. You're also signing a binding legal agreement that sets out various obligations which you'll have to fulfil. *Before you sign anything,* you must understand what those obligations are and be comfortable that you can do what will be required of you.

Help is at hand. The ASA has launched a low-cost law firm specifically for writers and illustrators, Authors Legal, which is available to all members. The report you receive will identify any legal issues and any areas where the commercial terms being offered differ significantly from the industry standard.

Otherwise, you can seek independent legal advice from an intellectual property lawyer. You *must* use a lawyer who has experience in the specialist area of author contracts; a general solicitor won't have the necessary experience to vet this type of agreement. The ASA also has on its website, a detailed template author agreement that can serve as a useful comparison to the contract you receive from your publisher.

MAJOR CLAUSES IN THE CONTRACT

If you don't have an agent negotiating on your behalf, it's essential that you understand the implications of the major clauses in a standard author agreement.

Copyright

It's vital that you appreciate the distinction between *licensing* and *assigning* your copyright. When you *license* your copyright, you're simply granting the publisher permission to use your copyrighted content in the languages, countries, formats and time frame that are specified in the contract. If you *assign* your copyright, however, you're transferring ownership of your copyright to the publisher, which is something you would only consider doing in certain circumstances, such as a commission to write for a one-off fee that offsets any royalty payments over the long term.

Term

The term means the period during which you're licensing your copyright to the publisher. Most publishers will start with the term set at the full length of copyright – the life of the author plus 70 years after death.

If you're reluctant to grant such a long licence, there are two ways you can deal with this:

1. Propose a set term, perhaps 10 years from first publication, which can be renewed upon mutual agreement. This may be difficult to achieve, particularly if you're a first-time author.
2. Ensure that the termination clause is reasonable (more on this shortly), because you must have a way of bringing the contract to an end if the publisher is no longer committed to your book.

Rights

Rights are the specific areas you're licensing to the publisher and are linked to the term, as that is the period for which those rights are being granted. The most obvious right is the right to publish your work, but you need to agree in what formats publication is permitted (print, eBook and audiobook are standard), for how long and in what countries? What about the right to translate your work into other languages or include your work in an anthology? What about the right to adapt your work for the stage or screen? Or serialise your work? Many publishers will attempt to secure a broad licence to all rights for the full period of copyright, but you don't have to agree to this and can try to negotiate some changes.

First, consider your publisher's ability to exploit the rights that they want to license. If they're a large multinational, they may have considerable experience in selling rights to international markets etc., but a small, relatively new publishing company is unlikely to have the necessary knowledge and contacts to exploit those rights effectively.

If you remain uneasy about granting all rights, you can try:

- To exclude some rights, e.g. you may have excellent merchandising contacts so you would prefer to retain full control of those rights
- To limit the time frame of some of the rights, e.g. include the international rights but only for a set time (somewhere between three and seven years), at the end of which the rights revert to you if the publisher has been unable to sell them
- To grant some rights on a non-exclusive basis, which leaves you free to also follow up any contacts that you may have.

The ASA's template author contract has a useful section that sets out the standard industry commercial terms, including the share of subsidiary rights that you should expect as an author, which is between 50/50 and up to 80/20 depending on the type of right and the publisher.

Royalties

Most authors are paid by way of royalties, which are a percentage of either the *retail* price excluding GST or the *net receipts,* which is the amount the publisher receives from the bookseller or the purchaser of the book. It's important to be very clear about the basis of payment for your royalties: the percentage of retail and net-based royalty rates should be very different as they are calculated from very different figures.

These are the print industry standards:

- 10% of retail price excluding GST, which would be $2.27 per book on a retail price of $24.95 ($22.68 after GST)
- 18%, or close to it, on a net receipt royalty. The same $24.95 book, excluding GST is $22.68. The bookseller receives an average of 45% discount off that price, so they pay the publisher $12.47 (the net receipt) and 18% of that is $2.24 per book.

If you confuse the two types of royalty and accept a royalty of 10% of net receipts rather than retail price, you will very significantly diminish your income. In the above example, for instance, your royalty would drop to $1.24 per book, meaning $1 less for you on every book sold.

You can also try and negotiate *escalators* or *risers* to these rates. This means that you get a higher royalty after your book has sold an agreed number of copies, e.g. at 10,000 copies your royalty might increase to 12.5% of retail price. As a first-time author, you have a reduced chance of achieving rising royalties, unless the publisher is paying you a significant advance, in which case you should try very hard to negotiate these higher royalties on sales that would exceed the publisher's expectations.

The digital industry standards are:

- 25% of net revenue has become the industry norm
- For an audiobook download, the same 25% of net receipt is becoming standard
- If an audiobook is to be sold in physical form, e.g. CDs, then the royalty ideally should reflect the rates paid on print books. Increasingly, however, physical sales are only made to libraries, in which case the standard is closer to 10% of net receipts.

There's another aspect of royalties that calls for vigilance: the *high discount* clause. The 'discount' referred to here is that granted by publishers to retailers. As was explained earlier, the standard discount of between 40 and 50% can be significantly higher when big retailers place a large order for a major new title. Independent retailers buying cooperatively can also negotiate better discounts.

A high discount royalty clause specifies that for sales made at or over a certain discount, the author's royalty reduces, usually from a rate of 10% of retail price to 10% of net receipts. The idea is that the publisher and author will share the reduced margin if a retailer places a large order at a higher than usual discount. This may be fine in principle, but the key to fairness is the discount threshold at which the change in royalty is triggered.

Many promotional purchases, where the retailer is buying a large volume to support an in-store promotion, would now receive a minimum of 50% discount, but for commercial titles that sell strongly in such places as department stores, the discounts on large orders can be much higher. Therefore a high discount clause that reduces the royalty rate at a discount under 55% can seriously disadvantage you.

The ASA recommends that authors are paid their standard royalty of 10% of retail price for all domestic sales where the discount to the retailer is 55% or lower. If you can negotiate for the threshold to be 60%, that's even better. You want to set the threshold discount as high as possible to ensure the greatest number of sales at your premium royalty, particularly if your book is a commercial title that will be heavily stocked by outlets that have negotiated a high discount.

Advance

This is an amount that the publisher is prepared to pay an author in advance of publication. In effect, it's a prepayment of a proportion of the royalties that the publisher is expecting to pay out on the first print run. The level of advance, or indeed the offer of any advance, varies significantly between publishers but, on average, is based on sales of anything from 30% to almost 100% of the anticipated royalties on the first printing, depending on the publisher's level of enthusiasm for your work. It therefore helps to know the publisher's publication plan, including the proposed quantity and retail price, to be able to assess the fairness of any advance you're being offered.

An advance is certainly helpful, but it isn't the only

factor to take into account in a publisher's offer: after all, it's only an advance on royalties that you'll earn anyway as the book sells. A large advance can even be a double-edged sword. It places high expectations on the book's performance and if those aren't met it may affect your chances of securing a second contract. You need to weigh up the degree to which you believe your publisher can maximise the sales of your work.

Example:

If we continue with our $24.95 book example, on standard terms you would earn $2.27 per book. If the planned first print run is 5,000 copies, you would earn $11,350 if every book sold. Depending on the size of the publisher and their enthusiasm for your work, you could therefore expect an advance of between $3,000 and $10,000.

Usually, advance payments are paid in instalments with a typical breakdown looking like this:

- One third on signing the contract
- One third on acceptance of your manuscript
- The final third on publication of your book.

Non-compete clause

There are many versions of this clause, but fundamentally its purpose is to prevent an author from writing a similar type of book during the term of the publishing agreement, thus undermining the sales of the current book. These clauses can be problematic, particularly for genre writers, such as crime and romance, or for non-fiction authors who are specialists in a particular field, because they have built their reputations by writing similar types of books. Wherever possible, it's best to try negotiating for this clause to be removed, but if this isn't possible, pay close attention to the way in which the clause is worded and the duration it specifies. The more specific the wording and the shorter the duration, the better.

Option clause

This clause is designed to give your publisher the first right of refusal on your next book. This isn't a problem if you've had a great experience with your first publication, but what happens if it hasn't gone very well and you have not established a strong relationship with your publisher? Given many publishers will agree to delete this clause, it's usually worth trying to have it removed, if you're concerned about being obligated in this way.

Warranties/obligations

You must understand your legal obligations and those of your publisher, so make sure that you read these sections carefully. In essence, you'll be undertaking that your work is original, that you haven't plagiarised anyone else's work and that you have permission for any copyrighted content you've used. You'll also be undertaking to deliver your work on time and at a publishable standard, and to participate in the editing and proofing stages of production in a timely and professional way.

The publisher will be undertaking to consult with you on the areas specified in the agreement, which usually include editing, proofing, cover design and blurb, although the final decision will be theirs since they pay for all costs of production, sales and marketing. They will also be obligated to publish your work in line with the agreed schedule and to report your sales and pay your royalties on the timetable set out in the contract.

Remember that your signature on the agreement confirms that you've read and understood what you're signing, so if you breach one of your obligations down the line, you can't turn around and plead ignorance. Read carefully.

Audit

This clause gives you the right, on written request, to examine your publisher's accounts of sales and royalty payments for your book. Such clauses usually allow for reimbursement of the cost of the inspection, as well as correcting any accounting error found, if it's above a certain percentage (often 5%). This is a very useful clause to add into your agreement: royalty accounting can be complex and mistakes easily made. If you ever become concerned that your royalty statements could be inaccurate, you'll be able to invoke this clause to make sure that all is well.

Termination/reversion

We touched on this when discussing the term of your agreement: you must have a mechanism to bring your agreement to an end if the publisher is no longer actively supporting your work. This used to be triggered if the book went out of print, but now that most books may remain available in perpetuity in their digital editions, the termination clauses have had to change. The contract does *not* automatically end and the rights revert to you when the book is out of print. It's up to you to write and request that the rights revert to you if the book is no longer selling.

Read your termination clause carefully to ensure you can bring your contract to an end if sales fall below a defined threshold. Reversion clauses should read something like this: 'After the first two years from date of publication of the Work, if fewer than x copies of the Work across all editions have been sold in a royalty accounting period and the Publisher fails to revive sales to this level within 6 months of having received written notice from the Author or their representative to do so, the Author may terminate this Agreement immediately by written notice.'

If the draft contract has no termination clause or includes one that is triggered only if the book goes out of print, you must negotiate to have an updated clause included in your agreement.

KEEP AN EYE OUT

Publication date

The date that the publisher plans to release your book, although they can change this at any time. If this date is critical to the success of the book, for example a high-profile promotional opportunity, it's vital that you deliver on time.

Delivery date

The date on which you're required to submit your final manuscript. Failure to deliver on time is often grounds for termination of the agreement. You can, however, often negotiate for a reasonable extension of time if necessary.

Acceptance date

This date is important because it signifies that the publisher has accepted not only that you've submitted your work, but that it fulfills all your obligations, and the publishing process can begin.

Additional material

Most agreements will specify that the author is responsible for sourcing all additional material, including quotes and illustrations, as well as securing permission to use them and payment of any fees. If your book is highly illustrated, you may want to talk to your publisher and see if you can negotiate a cap to your financial obligations, as permission fees to use images can be very expensive.

Design, format, cover

Although many contracts specify that the publisher will consult with the author on these matters, they will all state that the publisher makes the final decision, even if it differs from the author's view. You should, though, always have the opportunity to give your opinion and most publishers will do their best to accommodate your opinions wherever they can.

Correction of proofs

The contract will set out the turnaround time and the

number of changes you can make before you start having to pay for them. By the time you get to the final proofs, you should only be changing a typo, grammatical error or a factual mistake. If you start rewriting passages because you think they'll read better, this could become very costly.

Indemnity

This clause can seem intimidating, but it's there to ensure that you haven't plagiarised any of your content, used someone else's work without permission or defamed anyone. If you're writing a non-fiction work about real people, it's wise to discuss the mitigation of any defamation risk with your publisher before you sign your agreement.

Remainders

This is the industry term for excess stock. This clause should specify when a publisher can remainder your work (somewhere between 12 and 24 months after publication) and state their obligation to notify you in advance and give you the opportunity to buy as many copies as you would like at the remainder price. As a benchmark, the remainder price is in the region of 80% off the recommended retail price. If the books are being sold below cost, you don't receive a royalty on remaindered stock.

The art of negotiation

It can be difficult to negotiate effectively with a publisher, particularly if you're a first-time author. You'll be excited about the prospect of being published and may be concerned that if you rock the boat, you could risk losing the offer altogether. These fears are understandable, but no ethical publisher will walk away from a contract simply because you raise some matters for discussion; nor will they deny you the chance to obtain advice. They will walk away, however, if you're so inflexible and unreasonable that they no longer feel able to publish your book without unnecessary dissension.

So, do your homework and plan your negotiation carefully. Make a list of all the issues you'd like to raise with your publisher. Although the importance of certain clauses may differ depending on individual circumstances, trying to fit your concerns into the following categories will be helpful.

CRITICAL

These are aspects of the contract that could have a significant impact on either your earning power or your future career. Without some compromise from the publisher, it may be unwise to sign.

- ***Assignment/licence of copyright:*** For a trade publication, where your readers are general bookshop buyers, it's very important that you never *assign* your copyright unless exceptional circumstances prevail.
- ***Royalties below market rate:*** This would seriously erode your income, so you need to think very carefully about working with a publisher who doesn't offer rates close to or in line with industry standards.

- ***High discount royalty clause:*** The threshold set will be critical if you're a genre writer, and your primary market will be large mass market retailers.
- ***Termination clause:*** If your contract doesn't have a reasonable termination clause, you may find it impossible ever to extricate yourself or get your rights back. If the book is the first in a series, for instance, this could be a significant problem.

IMPORTANT

These are the matters that require serious discussion, but if you can't reach any compromise in your discussions you may be willing to still sign the contract, particularly if you have no other options or the publisher is such a good fit that you believe it's a risk worth taking.

- ***Term:*** A life of copyright licence is less concerning if the contract also has a fair termination clause. If it doesn't, you'll have no contractual means of bringing that agreement to end.
- ***Audit:*** No reputable publisher will ever try to manipulate your royalty payments, but many publishers have ageing royalty systems and mistakes do happen. This is therefore a very helpful clause to have in your contract and it's worth trying to include it.
- ***Non-compete:*** This is unlikely to trouble you if your work is a one-off, but if you're writing in a specific

genre or subject area, it's essential that you either get this clause removed, or moderated in duration.

- ***Share of subsidiary rights income:*** The ASA recommends authors try and achieve at least a 70% share, with 50% as the bare minimum.

NICE TO HAVE

These issues are worth airing and would be great to include, but aren't deal-breakers if the publisher stands firm:

- ***Option:*** Try to delete or at least negotiate the wording to make the clause as unrestrictive as possible, just in case.
- ***Advance:*** If you and your publisher fulfil the other requirements of your contract, you'll earn your maximum royalties, with or without an advance.
- ***Rising royalties:*** These may be difficult to negotiate for your first book, but if you have an established track record as an author, these are an excellent way of ensuring that you share in the success if your book sells well above expectation.

Ethical publishers will be willing to discuss any points you raise and depending on the changes you want to make, most will be willing to compromise on at least some. It's extremely unlikely that you'll reach a negotiation impasse with an experienced and respected publisher.

There are, however, many less ethical players in the market who purport to be publishers when they are, in fact, merely publishing services providers, and they can be very reluctant to negotiate and to adhere to industry standard terms. If you encounter such an attitude, it's worth researching your publisher more thoroughly; an early unwillingness to compromise bodes ill for the future. In such circumstances an expert contract review is very helpful: it will advise on when you need to draw the line and walk away.

CHILDREN'S AUTHORS AND ILLUSTRATORS

The standard contract for children's authors and illustrators is the same, but it's important to understand the way in which income is shared. If you're an established writer/illustrator pairing, the publisher may consider a joint contract, but often the contracts will be separate, although with the same obligations. In either instance, the industry norm is that the advance and all the royalty/rights revenue will be shared on a 50/50 basis between the two of you. This means that a royalty of 5% of retail price is standard for children's authors and illustrators. Keep a close eye on the high discount clause, however, as children's book clubs can buy at very high discounts. These orders can, however, help the publisher to build an economical print run and give your book great exposure in schools, so it's worth asking about this before you sign the agreement, so that you're fully informed before you commit.

For illustrators, a set fee may sometimes be offered

instead of a royalty. The ASA's recommended rates of pay for book illustration will give you some guidance on the size of appropriate fee, as will some of the other resources listed at the end of this book. If a fee is offered, be sure to check the copyright clause as the offer may involve an assignment of copyright to the publisher. If you're willing to contemplate this, you must be confident that the fee is sufficiently significant to forgo further income if the book goes on to do very well – and quality children's picture books can sell steadily for many years.

Publication

WHY DOES IT TAKE SO LONG?

Making your book is a slow process – at least 12 months on average from acceptance of your final manuscript through to publication. This can feel like an eternity and many authors find it difficult to understand why the production is so drawn out. There are, however, a number of good reasons for the timeline:

- Your book isn't the only title being made. Every publisher will have many books in production at the same time, even if they're at different stages in the process. Regardless of the size of the publisher, resources aren't limitless and even if freelancers are being used in both editorial and design, the in-house team will still be involved in management and quality control.

- Publishers take pride in the quality of their work, and some manuscripts require a considerable amount of editorial care and attention before they reach the required standard.
- The timeline isn't what it seems. To publish a manuscript delivered in March one year in the following March, finished stock has to be in the Australian distributor's warehouse by the end of January at the latest. This means that the final print files have to be sent to the printer before Christmas, if the book is being printed in Australia. If the title requires proof copies, these must be produced by the end of October, so they can be distributed and read before the sales team starts to sell-in to the booksellers. All of a sudden that 12-month lead time has reduced to between six and seven.
- Particularly if your book is a lead title, the marketing team needs time to prepare and implement the marketing plan and the sales team needs time to prepare their approach so they can enthuse the booksellers.

So you'll have to be patient. As we've seen, the publisher almost always has the final say on various production matters. This can be frustrating, but it's worth remembering that, unlike you, the publisher will have had many years' experience making high-quality books and positioning them correctly for their target market. It makes sense, therefore, to pick your battles. Make sure that you meet every deadline the editor sets for you to review editorial changes or approve proofs, and act reasonably. Try not to become white noise, so that if an issue arises that you feel very strongly about, you improve your chances of being heard.

THE FINISH LINE

The day will come, however, when you hold that finished copy in your hands and all the time and effort will recede in the face of that overwhelming sense of achievement. Now it's time to do everything you can to support your book.

Lead title

If you are one of the lucky ones with a lead title, your publisher has probably already introduced you to the sales team and possibly to some important booksellers, so they get excited about your book well before publication day. But before the stock is released to bookstores, the publicity and marketing plan will kick in, and you'll be assigned a publicist. This work can include a combination of:

- Media interviews, including radio, print and influential podcasts and blogs, even TV if your work is very high profile
- Anything from a nationwide author tour to signings in local bookshops, either as events or simply visiting the bookshops to meet the booksellers and sign their stock
- Public speaking at any relevant event or festival

- Opinion pieces in media outlets relevant to the subject matter of your book
- Guest social media appearances.

For some authors, this level of public speaking and media exposure can be very daunting, especially if they've never done it before. If you fall into this camp and are lying awake every night in dread, talk to your publicist. They will have the experience to guide you through the process, help you prepare for the questions that are likely to be asked, and if your book is very high profile or contentious, set up media training so that you feel able to face any difficult situations calmly and professionally.

Most of this activity will probably occur within the first four to six weeks after publication but, depending on the genre and sales of your book, the event work in particular could continue for longer than this. Although this is an excellent way to keep driving sales of your book, you need to consider the matter of payment. Events that are solely focused on the promotion of your book, especially when they're held close to the time of publication, have traditionally been unpaid, on the basis that your earnings will come by way of royalties.

If the events are more general, however, and not directly linked to publication, then it's fair to expect to be paid. If you're unsure about what to charge, the ASA publishes recommended rates of pay on their website. It can be difficult to strike the right balance between promotional work and professional event work, so if in doubt about whether it's reasonable to expect payment, ask your agent, talk to your publicist or an experienced author contact, or seek advice from the ASA.

Further down the list

Most titles aren't leads, and don't attract the same level of publicity and marketing support, or for as long. You may not get all the bells and whistles, but make sure you talk to your publisher well ahead of the book's release to clarify what support they can give and reassure them that you'll do anything that will help get the word out to your target market. There are also steps that you can take:

- Contact the bookstores in your local area (your publisher will be able to help with this) and offer to come in and either do a signing session or at least sign stock for them
- Mine your contact list and make sure that everyone knows about your book's publication
- If your book has a specific market, especially for non-fiction, make sure that your publisher has all those contact details so that they can send out free copies along with a press release
- Offer to speak at any event that may be happening in your area of interest
- If you have a social media presence, draw on that expertise and spread the word

- If you have media contacts who might be interested in opinion pieces or blog/podcast spots, follow them up.

This is not a time to hold back. You are your book's best advocate, and your publisher will help, wherever they can, through their direct access to the bookseller network and their excellent media lists. Always carry a copy of your book with you: you never know when the opportunity may arise for you to press it into the hands of someone with influence. The more positive word of mouth you can generate, the more likely it is that sales will grow.

All of this can, though, be challenging for many authors, especially first-timers, who are not accustomed to attracting attention. It can certainly be dispiriting, but don't give up. However wonderful it would be, your book doesn't need to be a bestseller. Your aim is to help achieve decent sales of the first print run, without excessive returns, in order to create a solid sales base for your next book.

Author power

The tough part about publishing a book, particularly for the first time, is that the balance of power lies with the publisher. They have the experience, knowledge and skill, and they take the financial risk. Most established publishers work closely and harmoniously with their authors and any problems are almost always the result of human error, and are easily fixed. There are, however, some very small, new companies that lack the experience, systems and cash flow to efficiently manage the complexities of publishing. There are also publishing services businesses positioning themselves as traditional publishers, which make their money from producing your book but have little or no interest in the ongoing success of your work. Their lack of attention after publication can be problematic.

But there are areas of the publishing process where authors can and should take control of their own destiny.

ROYALTY STATEMENTS

Your royalty statement is your payslip, but many authors don't understand, and therefore don't check, their statements thoroughly. In many ways this is understandable. There's little consistency in these statements across the industry and many are confusingly set out and sometimes incomplete. This is because royalty payments have become more complex, with a variety of new sales channels and formats, and many publishers' systems are struggling to cope.

Most publishers provide six-monthly sales accounting, usually calculated at the end of June and the end of December, and the statements and payments are made within 90 days. The current cumbersome process of preparing these payments is the reason for this long delay.

Regardless of the challenges publishers may face, it is incumbent on you, as the author, to thoroughly check every statement. Always keep your publishing contract filed with your royalty statements so that you can easily refer to previous statements and that all-important source document.

Key areas to check are:

- ***Your advance:*** Make sure you know the amount of your advance and check your previous statement to verify that the balance showing on your advance is correct.

- ***Returns provision:*** As we've seen, almost all books are sold to retailers on a sale or return basis. In an effort to avoid paying royalties on copies that may later be sent back, the returns provision allows the publisher to withhold a certain percentage of your earnings over the heaviest returns period, which is usually within the first six to 12 months of publication. Make sure that both the percentage and the period of the retention match your contract, and if actual returns have been less than the percentage, that the money withheld is released according to the contract. Many publishers won't exercise the returns provision if sales are strong, but if they choose to do so and you know your book is selling well, it's worth asking your publisher to waive the provision.

- ***High discount sales:*** These can be concerning, particularly if your book has strong commercial/mass market appeal. Your revenue from each high discount sale can halve the royalty you would receive on normal discount sales. If you're surprised by the level of high discount sales, query this with your publisher.

- ***Gratis:*** Bearing in mind that you receive no royalty on gratis copies, it's best to query this line if the number of gratis copies is high and you don't know of any reason for this.
- ***Subsidiary rights:*** If foreign rights income pops up that you know nothing about, or there's no explanation of the territory from which it has come, or indeed any other form of rights income is listed without explanation, ensure that you find out the details of the payment.

If you see anything on your statement that you don't understand, such as the balances brought forward seem odd, or deductions are listed without a reason being given, or there is a special sale that you know nothing about at a low per unit price, then ask for an explanation. You don't have to be accusatory or aggressive, but it's critical that you understand why you're being paid what you're being paid. Large publishers will be generating thousands of royalty statements in each royalty period, and it's incredibly easy for errors to slip in.

If you've exhausted every avenue and remain unconvinced about the accuracy or fairness of your royalty statement, then check your contract to see if it includes an audit clause.

Reputable publishers will be diligent about their reporting requirements but some authors still experience problems with less organised or ethical providers, either about getting timely statements or receiving the money they're owed. If you have this problem, you can:

- Contact your publisher and request that they provide your statement
- If no statement is sent, try again and request a response by a set date
- Write to the Australian Publishers Association, if your publisher is a member. Non-payment of royalties is a breach of their code of conduct, and they may be able to intervene on your behalf.
- If this doesn't result in action, try phoning and/or write a sterner letter, advising that failure to respond within seven days will force you to take further action.
- If you're still unsuccessful, contact the ASA through their free member advice service or seek legal advice from Authors Legal, or the Arts Law Centre of Australia, or a legal firm with expertise in publishing. You'll need to consider whether legal advice will cost you more than the value of the royalties you seek to recover, but sometimes a well-argued letter from a professional can solve the problem without the need for further expensive intervention.

DEATHLY SILENCE

The relentlessness of the monthly new title publishing program forces publishers to move on to the next set of new releases very quickly. It certainly isn't personal, but it can be difficult not to feel abandoned if your publisher falls silent. It's likely, however, that you'll have built relationships within the publishing team, so you can contact one of them to put your mind at rest. They may be reluctant to provide detailed sales information but will be able to give some feedback and reassurance. If, however, you have no contact for an extended period, it's perfectly acceptable to write to the publisher in charge and politely request an update.

BOOKSELLER FEEDBACK

This is a slightly fraught area, as no publisher wants to be contacted every time a member of your family goes into a store to buy your book, only to be told it's out of stock. But if you see copies being unexpectedly sold at remainder prices, or you know that there's still demand for your book, and the databases show that it's out of stock/out of print, it's sensible to talk to your publisher without making accusations.

ONGOING MARKETING

Some books may not sell in large volumes, but they can have a long and steady backlist life. If you can continue to generate marketing support by way of public appearances or social media opportunities, make sure to tell your publisher what you're doing. They'll be willing to support your initiatives, helping you to make stock available at an event, or providing free copies to key decision makers. You need to be reasonable about this, of course, and not contact them on a weekly basis, but they've invested time and money in your book and are genuinely committed to its success.

REVERSION

Remember, your rights revert to you *only* at your instigation. Many authors believe that when their book has stopped selling and there are no print copies available, the rights automatically revert to them. This is *not* the case.

If you've exhausted every option to stimulate sales and you consider that your publisher is no longer actively supporting your work, reversion of rights may be your best option. Start by checking the termination clause in your agreement. Typically, you can't terminate a publishing agreement within the first two or three years without the publisher's consent, but after that initial period, reversion becomes possible if certain conditions are met.

You'll need to follow whatever procedure for termination is specified in your contract, which usually sets out a sales threshold across all editions that must be met if the publisher wants to retain rights. If the publisher has clearly not met the criteria, you can then write a letter invoking that clause and asking your publisher to terminate the agreement and revert the rights to you. If the publisher wishes to retain their rights in your work, they will need to actively start selling your book again to meet the sales target within the specified period. You can find a sample reversion letter on the ASA website.

Even if your contract either lacks a termination clause or contains one based on the notion of 'in print', you may still contact your publisher and outline the problem. If your royalty statements demonstrate that your sales are below a more contemporary termination clause criterion, your publisher will probably still agree to revert rights.

It's also worth understanding that although you own the copyright of the text, the publisher has created the designed book, so they own the print-ready PDF because they have done all the editing, proofing and designing. They can't do anything with it, because they can't use your text, and many will either sell the file to you at a nominal cost or give it to you. It's therefore worth raising this when you discuss reversion, as it means that you could readily reprint the book yourself if you wanted to.

WHAT'S NEXT?

The answer to this question is as complex as the publishing process. Your next steps will be determined by many factors, including the level of success you've enjoyed, your reasons for writing in the first place, your personal circumstances and the state of the market. Some writers have a burning desire to bring a certain issue to the world's attention and publishing that book may be enough. But many authors feel that they can no more stop writing than they can stop breathing.

If your book has met the publisher's salesexpectations or has settled into a steady pattern of sale as a backlist title, it's more than likely that they'll be keen to acquire your next work, in which case, you can negotiate a new contract and start writing.

For many, however, the outcome may have been underwhelming and the publisher isn't rushing back to the negotiating table. This is when things get tricky. Although having real-time sales data is a helpful tool, particularly for publishers to manage their reprints more efficiently, the downside for authors is that any publisher can check the sales for any title, including yours. If those sales are lacklustre, their enthusiasm will start to wane. And those sales can also curb the enthusiasm of other publishers, potentially affecting your ability to take your work elsewhere.

At this point, it's sensible to examine the publishing process, particularly if you received good reviews, but disappointing sales:

- Was the book published at the right time? For instance, books can get lost in the deluge of new titles that are released for the Christmas market.
- Was it priced correctly in comparison with other similar titles?
- Was the format and cover right for the genre?
- As far as you could tell, was it on display in the right bookshops and in the right area of those shops?

- Did you receive the promised publicity?

It's always much easier to see any mistakes after the event, but it's important to figure out if factors other than the book itself caused the poor result. Sometimes it's simply a combination of bad luck – another very similar book published at the same time, or some well-intentioned, but wrong calls by the publisher. If the publisher agrees that your book sales were affected by circumstances beyond your control, they may well be prepared to consider your second book.

But if you can't identify any such reasons, it's sensible to pause and examine your reasons for writing:

- If writing brings you joy, then focus on your writing and forget about publishing for a while as you hone your skills
- If you want to continue building a career as a writer, then you also need to focus on your writing skills and forget about publishing for a while. Writing a wonderful new book is your best chance of stimulating your flagging career
- If it's a burning desire to articulate a cause or an issue, why not consider other alternatives, such as blogs, either your own or contributing to specialist established outlets, articles, podcasts or any other new digital channel
- If it's fame and fortune, it's important to realise this is exceptionally rare in the book industry.

We've all heard the stories about the first-time writer who becomes an overnight sensation, but there would be a handful of these success stories worldwide in any given year, and many of those authors would still have work languishing in the bottom drawer. John Grisham's novel *The Firm* burst onto the international scene, going on to sell more than 7 million copies. Most people think it was his first book, but in fact this slot was taken by *A Time to Kill*, a book inspired by a real trial. After many, many rejections from both publishers and agents, the book was finally published with a print run of 5,000 copies, which in those days was tiny for the US. Grisham then purchased 1,000 copies of that print run, put them in the back of his car and toured the country in a bid for both promotion and sales. This book only sold millions of copies after Grisham had become a household name. So even the rare overnight successes aren't always what they seem.

Writing well needs more than flair and talent: it requires practice, receptiveness to knowledgeable feedback and self-discipline. It also requires an author to read.

"Read, read, read. Read everything... trash, classics, good and bad, and see how they do it. Just like a carpenter who works as an apprentice and studies the master. Read! You'll absorb it. Then write...". William Faulkner

Stephen King put it even more bluntly, "If you don't have time to read, you don't have the time (or the tools) to write. Simple as that."

So if you don't want to abandon your dream of a writing career, and you have the means and opportunity to pursue that dream, you must read, practise, ask for feedback from professionals and keep building your experience. Other than the very rare prodigy, a violinist doesn't toss off Beethoven's violin concerto soon after they first picked up the instrument. Why should great writing be any different?

Getting published is hard, but it always has been. The difference now is that writing has shifted from being the domain of a smaller group of people with the education, time and resources to devote to it, to being something possible for anyone with basic computer skills. The love of writing has become synonymous with publishing. But despite all the obstacles, good books usually shine through. Fashion plays its part as trends come and go, as does luck, and it can take time and a large dose of resilience, but if you have genuine feedback from the right people that your work is of publishable quality, keep going. Read widely, watch the market and practise, practise, practise.

PART 3

PART 3

Author-funded publishing

Growth in self-publishing

Over the last 20 years, advances in technology have made it possible for anyone with access to the internet to publish a book. Before this, businesses that advertised for authors to submit their work and pay for publication were known as vanity presses. Because they made little effort to edit or improve the work in any way, and took shortcuts in production, the books they produced were usually of poor quality and 'vanity press' became a pejorative term.

Since the technological transformation much of the negativity associated with vanity publishing has gone, although the plethora of sub-standard self-published work stops the stigma from disappearing altogether. Hence the range of terms that now replace vanity publishing, including self-publishing, independent publishing, hybrid publishing, contributory publishing, custom publishing and author-funded publishing.

It's difficult to determine exactly how many books are published in this way, other than by way of the number of ISBNs issued by Thorpe Bowker for both print and digital formats. In the US, Bowker conducts an annual survey, and their 2019 results showed an increase of 40% over the previous year, a total of 1.6 million ISBN registrations. This wasn't far off half of the total ISBN registrations in 2019. This staggering number demonstrates just how many people want to be published authors.

Several factors have caused this rapid growth:

1. Changes in technology have both simplified and reduced the costs of book production, broadened formats and opened up new channels of sale. Amazon has made it possible for anyone to be a publisher. EBooks and print-on-demand technology have also made it possible to publish without incurring the prohibitive cost of a large print run
2. The rise in popularity of the belief that there's a book in everyone (more on this shortly)
3. The increasing difficulty in securing an agent and/or a traditional publisher
4. The lure of greater financial return and control for the author
5. A lack of understanding of the publisher's role, with the term publisher often being used interchangeably with printer.

Such runaway successes as *Fifty Shades of Grey*, with sales of 125 million copies in under four years, have naturally raised the hopes of legions of self-published authors, but the prospect of retaining 70% of the revenue, as opposed to 10% of the retail price, is also a powerful motivator. There are now many companies set up to reap the rewards of this change, from publishing services businesses to those promoting self-growth through publishing.

Everyone may have a story, and often an intriguing and interesting one, but this does *not* mean that it can or should become a book. It's possible for almost everyone to write, but it's not possible for everyone to make money from their writing. Enjoyment of writing has become synonymous with the belief that the writer deserves to be published. They may dream about it, but not every amateur artist expects to have their work hung in a gallery. This huge rise in participation and expectation has created a very cluttered market, making it ever more difficult for a new book to be found, even if it is worth reading.

For most authors, the traditional publishing path remains their preferred option and most, but by no means all, authors funding their own publication have taken that route out of necessity rather than choice. As already mentioned, the exceptions to this generalisation are genre writers, authors who have already built a strong community around their area of expertise and previously published writers with a loyal following.

If you and your work fall into one of those categories, if you want to publish a book purely for family and friends, or if you've tried every possible path to traditional publishing and failed to place your work, despite a positive, professional assessment, then funding your own publication may well be worthwhile.

Don't forget, however, that making the book is the easy part. There are good publishing services companies and many excellent freelancers, who can help you produce a high-quality print and digital book that will be indistinguishable from a traditionally published title. The challenge lies in discoverability and accessing sales channels: How do people know about your book and where can they buy it?

What makes a book sell?

If you're contemplating funding your own publication, it's important to understand the qualities that define a saleable book.

First and foremost, of course, is the content. In fiction, whether literary or mass market, and whatever the genre, the standard of writing, the intricacies of the plot, the depth of characterisation and how much the reader cares about those characters, all work together to make a satisfying and absorbing book. For non-fiction, too, whatever the subject, the writing must be good, the subject matter gripping and the research impeccable.

Understanding your genre and the market for whom you're writing is critical (this includes reading widely in that genre before you even begin to write.) The public aren't easily fooled and devotees of genres, such as crime and romance, have a sophisticated understanding of how good examples of those genres work. You underestimate their discernment at your peril.

Bad content that is packaged beautifully won't last the distance but wonderful content that has been badly produced may never take flight. It's therefore critically important that a good book is well edited and well laid out. The cover must be striking and in keeping with the genre and the blurb must compel the reader to make a purchase. You must understand your audience and understand what they're looking for.

It's difficult to obtain accurate data on eBook sales, but most industry pundits estimate that, on average, a new eBook sells between 150 and 300 copies. The sad truth behind this statistic is that most of the titles being published aren't of publishable standard and lack the commercial appeal necessary to generate worthwhile sales. It's disappointing to have your book fail in the marketplace, whichever way you choose to publish, but it's so much worse if you've put your time and hard-earned money behind its production.

Given the importance of content, it's worth reiterating, as pointed out in Part I, that before you start to incur the costs of publication it's wise to have your work assessed by an expert. Of course, it's possible to produce an eBook quickly and easily, but it won't attract an audience if the content is sub-standard and disappointing.

Authors often prefer to use beta readers to help them hone their work. This can be a useful tool, but it's still dependent on the skills, knowledge and experience of those readers. If you simply circulate your work to well-meaning family and friends, you're not going to receive objective comments, partly because they won't want to hurt your feelings, but also because they may be reading outside their realm of experience, making their comments irrelevant or unhelpful. Whichever way you choose to have your work appraised, make sure you send it to the right people

If you receive a positive assessment from a good assessor, it will encourage you to continue down the author-funded path, but if the critique concludes that your work isn't at the required standard, listen and consider alternatives such as printing a few copies for family and friends because it is your money on the line.

Developing your publishing plan

It's now time to explore exactly what you're trying to achieve with your book, so that you can make an informed decision about which self-publishing route is right for you. This process is akin to the acquisition proposal that a publisher would prepare. In essence you're scoping out the parameters of your book, including everything from the right format to the appropriate retail price, so you can produce a book that will appeal to your audience.

GOAL

The first step in any plan is to clarify what you are trying to achieve.

- Fame and fortune?
- Cost recovery and steady sales?
- Enhancement of your reputation?
- A calling card for your business?
- A memento for family and friends?

Most authors don't have unlimited resources, so determining your key driver will help you to establish how much time and money you're willing to invest in your publishing project.

TARGET MARKET

It's essential to research your target market before the publication of your book because, just like in a publishing house, the information you gather should inform key decisions: the cover and book design, the format, the title, the blurb, the pricing and so on.

To define your target market you'll want to find out the following about your readers:

- Gender?
- Age?
- Where do they buy their books?
- How do they find out about the books they want to buy?

- Whose opinion do they trust?

Most authors write in a genre they personally enjoy, so thinking about your own answers to these questions is a good place to start your research.

Once you've defined your market, study your competition to find answers to these questions:

- What format/s are best suited to your readership: print and/or digital?
- If the answer is digital, on which platforms do your readers buy their books?
- If your readers prefer print books, where do they buy: mass market stores, independent bookshops or online?
- What price points seem to be the most popular?
- Is there a better time of the year to publish?
- What style of covers dominate? What layout best suits the genre?

When you've gathered this information, you'll have all the elements needed to brief the services company or freelancers who will work with you to produce your book, and to inform your marketing and promotion strategy.

YOUR RESPONSIBILITIES

Before we start to examine your options in more depth, there are some details that, in your role as publisher of your book, you'll need to manage.

ISBN

Always buy your own ISBN and barcode and use your own imprint on your work. Your print and eBook editions will each need a separate ISBN and barcode, as will an audiobook if you're planning to produce one. This can be done very easily online at Thorpe Bowker at a cost of $45. Many service providers charge $100+ for this service, which is not only unnecessary, but creates a problem: if that provider prints stock using their imprint, ISBN and barcode, and you decide to stop working with them, you may not be able to sell those print copies because they carry the branding of that services company. It's much better to go your own way.

Legal deposit

One copy of every Australian publication must be deposited with the National Library of Australia and with your local state library, either in print or digital format. This is very easy to do online. You'll find the instructions on the websites of both institutions.

Copyright Agency

If there is any chance that your book may be copied or shared in schools, libraries or the workplace, you should join the Copyright Agency. They administer the educational and government statutory licences and also have licence arrangements in place with businesses, and distribute income from these licences. It's easy to join online.

Lending rights

Public Lending Rights (PLR) and Educational Lending Rights (ELR) payments are also worthy of your attention. This is a scheme whereby eligible authors receive a per-unit payment for the number of copies of their print book held in public and/or educational libraries, by way of compensating them for sales lost through public lending. You can find more information on the website of the Office for the Arts.

ABN/GST

If you are funding and selling your own book, you should register for an Australian business number (ABN). This is free and easy to do online. You then need to work out if you are required to register for goods and services tax (GST). This is explained in detail on the Australian Tax Office (ATO) website.

Tax deductions

As a self-employed person, there may be expenses associated with your work that you can claim as deductions in your tax return. Talk to either your accountant or bookkeeper, or visit the ATO website for guidance.

Option A: Do it yourself

As we saw in the Choosing the Right Publishing Path chart on page 64, you have a choice of two major routes for producing your own book, and the first is to handle the process yourself.

The DIY option means that you project manage the production of your own book, potentially using the same freelance editors and designers who work for traditional publishers. This approach allows you to control the costs, quality and timeline. It can be a daunting undertaking, particularly for a first-time author, but it's certainly not impossible if you work through the process logically and are realistic about your resources.

POTENTIAL WIP COSTS

Before you start sourcing potential freelancers, it's important to be aware of the costs you can expect to incur, especially because these can vary widely depending on the length of your manuscript, the standard of your writing, the level of skill and experience of the person/s working on your book and the result you're seeking.

These are called the work in progress (WIP) costs and cover everything you need to do to turn your manuscript into a print-ready PDF/digital file. If you plan to publish in eBook format only, depending on how you're going to make it available on the major retail platforms, there may be a small additional charge to convert the files into all the standard formats required.

If you want to achieve a high-quality book of the same standard as one that has been traditionally published, the indicative costs for a text-only title of 70,000–80,000 words would be:

Editing:	$1,000–$2,000+ depending on the amount of work required
Proofreading:	$600
Cover design:	$1,000–$2,000+
Layout files:	$750
ISBN and barcode:	$45
TOTAL:	Between $3,395 and $5,395+

If your manuscript requires significant structural work, these editorial and proofing costs could be considerably higher.

POTENTIAL PRINT COSTS

If your plan is to sell in both print and digital formats, you must also take your print costs into account. These vary considerably, depending on the size of the print run. Smaller digital printings will cost more per unit than longer print runs on a printing press (offset printing) but will carry much less risk because the total cost and stock holding are lower.

Given the number of variations in book specifications, it's difficult to provide a fair benchmark figure for printing, but to provide some perspective, publishing services provider IngramSpark's print and ship calculator for a standard format, text-only book is as follows:

Specifications:

- C format (234 x 156 mm) paperback
- Crème paper
- Perfect bound (glued spine with matt laminate colour cover)
- 198 pages
- 100 copies
- Shipping to Sydney

Costs: $663.07, which includes the shipping cost of $30.87. A per unit cost of $6.63. This is known as short-run printing.

Print-on-demand means that you print to order, so if you receive an order for one copy, you print and send that single unit. The costs per unit change significantly, however, because of the expense of shipping just one book. The same specifications, for a single copy, will cost $22.95 per unit because the delivery cost will be more than $14.

If you were to print offset, you could significantly lower the per-unit print price if you printed 3,000 copies, to potentially under $3, but your total print investment would rise to nearly $9,000, significantly increasing your risk. You would also have thousands of books to store and sell.

In summary, the same book will cost approximately:

- $22.95 per unit as a one-off print-on-demand copy
- $6.63 per unit for a short run of 100 copies
- $3 per unit for a 3,000-offset printing job.

GETTING PROFESSIONAL HELP

The professional associations are an excellent place to start searching for well-qualified freelancers to assist with your WIP costs. Both the Australian Book Designers Association and the Institute of Professional Editors have directories of freelancers, with short biographies that detail their areas of speciality and levels of experience.

Some published books also list the designer on the imprint or title page or on the back, so if you have a favourite cover or two, you may also be able to discover some skilled designers this way. It's slightly more difficult to find an editor this way, since their hard work is not as visible as a cover, but a name that comes up often is a strong indication of quality, and reviewing the acknowledgements section of a book can also be useful. You should bear in mind, however, that good freelancers are very much in demand, and you may have to wait to be able to secure their services.

When it comes to printing, there are good book printers based in Australia, which offer very competitive rates for short-run and offset text-only books. Potential mainstream book printers are Griffin Press, Ligare and SOS Print + Media Group.

If you're envisaging a full-colour illustrated coffee table book, however, overseas printing, despite the additional freight, will be much more cost effective for a print run of 3,000 copies or more. Because of the production technicalities involved in this type of printing, it would be worth considering using a print broker to help you with the complex specifications these books require and to organise the printing on your behalf. A couple of options are Imago and Small But Mighty Productions.

If you're printing a children's picture book, you can do short-run printing in Australia, but your choice of format and paper stock may be more limited, and it can be difficult to produce the book to the same standard as offset printing. You could potentially test the market with a small print run in your local area and then move to a larger offset run if the results warrant that level of investment.

EBOOK

The process for making an eBook is identical to that of a print book, until the final stage of the process, when the print-ready PDF has to be converted to ePub, for most digital retail platforms. A variety of companies can manage this conversion for you, but most of them also act as aggregators to manage your eBooks across the major retail platforms. We'll discuss these options under the other publishing services businesses section.

If you want to convert your files yourself and manage the retail platforms from there, there are a range of online convertors. Alternatively, some of the aggregators do offer conversion only, such as IngramSpark, at a cost of 60 cents per page.

AUDIOBOOK

Audiobooks have boomed in recent years, as smart phones have allowed us to listen anywhere, anytime. And advances in technology have brought down the costs of production. There are still some challenges for self-published authors in this area of the market, but it's becoming increasingly accessible.

As with eBooks, you can create the audio book yourself, or you go with a provider who will produce the audio and then make it available on retail platforms. Because they're concerned about their lack of understanding of the format, and the likely costs involved, most authors use one of the services companies, but if you want to give it a go yourself, here are a few tips.

The first step is to find the person who will narrate your book. If your book is non-fiction, you may decide to do this yourself, particularly if you have experience as a speaker in your specialist area, but if you've written a novel, you'll almost certainly need an experienced voice actor. The best way to find one is through agents such as EM Voices, RMK Voices and Scout Talent. The first two are professional agencies specialising in voice-over actors, but some self-published authors have used the services of Scout Talent.

Using your brief, think carefully about how the audio needs to fit your book and then listen to samples of potential voices and make a choice. It's difficult to estimate costs as these will depend on the experience of the person selected and the length of the book being read, but you can consult the recommended rates at Media and Entertainment and Arts Alliance (MEAA). For a narrator without a high profile, the minimum standard is $125 per finished hour.

On average a 70,000-word book will translate to 7.5 finished hours as an audio book, based on Audible's rate of 9,300 words per finished hour of audio. This means that the cost of the narration would be around $1,000 to $2,000, but this could go up to as much as $5,000 if you pay a flat rate to an actor with a profile.

The next step is to produce the recording, which is dependent on quality equipment and an appropriate studio. Although many people now record podcasts themselves, audiences expect a much higher quality for an audio book. If you don't have any experience in this area, it would be much wiser to use the services of professionals. Magic Studios in Perth, and Brisbane Audiobook Production offer these services, although you'll need to conduct your own research about these and other options. Again, it's difficult to determine exact costs, but an estimate would be $3,000 for the studio production time for a work of this length.

DIY SUMMARY

Controlling the entire production process can be an appealing prospect, but it's not for the faint-hearted. The costs vary significantly, largely based on the way in which you handle the print edition. If you decided to produce an eBook only, your investment could be around the $3,000 level, up to as much as $14,500 if you added a 3,000-copy print run. An audiobook will add somewhere in the vicinity of $5,000. Many authors, however, overestimate how many copies they're likely to sell and end up losing money. Never print your book before you've worked out in detail where and how you're going to sell it and make sure that you thoroughly research the potential for your digital sales. More on this after we've examined the second self-publishing option.

Option B: Publishing services companies

As technology has advanced, so too have the number of potential authors and 'publishing' companies keen to make the most of this potential new income source. Unlike traditional publishers, who make money only if a book sells, publishing services businesses make their money upfront from invoicing you for the services they've provided. They therefore have no, or low, vested interest in the levels of sales that the book generates.

For the many authors who don't feel confident about their ability to manage the book production process on their own, however, the prospect of handing this work over to a publishing services business is appealing.

PUBLISHING SERVICES BUSINESSES EXPLAINED

Three different types of publishing services companies are available to you.

1. Traditional publishers. There are two ways in which traditional publishing companies venture into author-funded publishing:
    - A small number have a separate self-publishing division, where the authors fund their own books, but the publisher provides services, and sometimes distribution, at the same professional level as the rest of their business
    - Small underfunded independent publishing companies look to the author to partly support the financing of the publication by paying for certain production costs, such as editing, or by agreeing to purchase a set number of finished copies to provide cash flow and some certainty for the print run.
2. Publishing services companies that clearly state the services they provide and the costs of each of those services. They don't require you to sign an author contract, just a service agreement setting out what they will do and what and when you'll pay them to do it.

3. Publishing services businesses that describe themselves as publishers, sometimes with a qualifier such as hybrid, contributory, joint venture or partnership. Although these companies are charging fees for service, they often adopt contracts that substantially mirror traditional publishing contracts, including, for example, an exclusive copyright licence and royalty accounting provisions. Concerningly, some services make claims about their sales and distribution capacity that range from optimistic to hyperbolic.

Option 1 has advantages, particularly the traditional publisher offering professional services, since you'll achieve a high-quality book and sometimes, access to market as well, but it is an expensive alternative that many authors cannot afford. The part-funded alternative with an independent small publisher can work well, but seek further assurance about the company's financial stability before entering into such an agreement, and do your homework about their distribution channels and marketing capacity.

Option 2 is the most affordable and transparent alternative, if you can find a publishing services provider with the skills and knowledge to produce a high-quality publication at a fair price. The crucial issue, however, is how to work out which companies are reliable and which ones fall into the potentially problematic category outlined in the third option.

RED FLAGS AND HOW TO RECOGNISE THEM

Many authors, eager to see their book dream realised, shortcut their research and rush into a decision about a service provider without proper consideration. Although there may seem to be a bewildering number of choices available, many can be quickly dismissed if you're alert to the signs that distinguish the bad and the ugly from the good and trustworthy.

Anonymity

Many sites claim to have a team of highly experienced publishing professionals but none of these people are named, and their qualifications and experience aren't listed. A reputable site, on the other hand, will generally be only too pleased to highlight their team's publishing credentials.

A sub-standard website

Why would you want to produce a book with a business that hasn't taken the time to fix the poor spelling and grammar on their own website?

Lack of transparency

If the services on offer and the fees for those services aren't clearly stated on a company's website or, at the very least, easily obtained, proceed with great caution. A reputable services company will have no problem being transparent about their offer.

Appropriation of the term 'publisher'

Many problematic service companies describe themselves as a publisher and use many publishing terms and conditions that are inappropriate when you, as the author, are paying for all the costs of making and selling your book. Unless you're actually dealing with a publisher, it's both inappropriate and unnecessary to exclusively license your copyright to a provider. Do *not* sign any agreement without seeking advice.

Solicitation

If the company has initiated contact, be very wary. Traditional publishers and ethical publishing services businesses have no need to cold call in order to get clients.

Extravagant or unsubstantiated claims

The range of these is broad, but includes claims about worldwide sales, international marketing reach, which usually means that your title will be one of many millions listed on international bibliographic databases. Unless it's obvious that the business has its own sales and marketing team, it's highly unlikely that your book will receive any attention after publication.

Take your time and read the websites carefully. Examine the books previously published by that provider as closely as you can, reading the blurbs and analysing the covers. You want to be absolutely certain that you'd be happy to have that company make your book before you contemplate taking the next step.

SERVICES

You get what you pay for. The red flags above will help you to avoid the worst of the services companies, but you can narrow your choices down further by learning to read between the lines of the often carefully constructed list of services. The description of the services on offer and the associated costs are also excellent indicators of the professionalism and skill of the provider.

Editing

A good editor will do a quick read of the full manuscript first, to get a sense of the flow of the work and to identify where there are problems with plot or character and then they'll return to the beginning and go through it again, making proposed changes or raising questions throughout the work. This takes time. On average an adult reads at a speed of somewhere between 200 and 250 words per minute, meaning that an average-sized novel would take at least five hours for that initial read alone. Therefore, even a relatively clean manuscript will take at least 15 hours to edit, after that initial read.

Many services businesses don't even list editing as one of the services on offer, but if they do, the attributed cost for that service, or the total cost of the package, will reveal that they'll do nothing more than a very swift tidy-up of glaring typos using a spell checker, not a professional edit.

Typesetting/internal design

Good internal design is another skilled task, so once again, read the description of the service with care. Sub-standard operators are merely dumping the finished text into a standard template, with little regard for page or chapter breaks.

Cover design

This can be an easier area to assess as many companies show their previous work on their websites. This means that you can look carefully to determine if they're simply using standard templates and free stock photos. This type of cover will not compete with professionally designed books and is often the first sign that the book has not been well produced.

Distribution

If this is included in a package without any mention of a sales team or a warehouse, it almost always means that your book will be listed on major bibliographic databases. Technically, a retailer wanting to order your book could find it, but given the multiple millions of titles on these databases, the chances of that happening are almost nil, unless a customer were to place an order with that retailer.

Marketing

Generally, look for specificity: exactly what activities does the company's marketing and publicity entail?

Beware of the terms 'kit', 'advice' and 'mentoring'. Not one of these descriptors means that the company will provide tangible marketing for your book: they will simply give you some standard information that you could find yourself with a quick internet search.

The same holds true for the promise of book or author videos. These are invariably very basic and of little practical benefit, unless you have a broad social media reach and can put such collateral to good use, as the provider doesn't usually offer distribution of these.

Press releases, too, will be very generic and of no practical benefit because such providers very rarely send these out to a database *tailored to your book.*

Promotional material can also be on offer, but hard-copy fliers and posters are useless to you unless you've managed to get your book into bricks and mortar bookshops.

Website

The more expensive packages often include creating an author website, but check whether this just means a standard template landing page that almost anyone could build quickly using free software. These packages are offering nothing you need or have asked for and you will not achieve a better book as a result. Is this a good use of your money?

COSTS

The final aspect you need to consider before making your decision is cost. The price of these packages varies considerably, but often starts between $1,000 and $2,000 (either with no printed books, or a handful of copies only), up to $15,000–$20,000 at the most exclusive end. Many services companies package their services using a ranking system such as gold, silver and bronze, with extra services added at each level. Many of those, however, are merely window dressing. The additional cost in the high-end packages usually relates to the inclusion of around 1,000 print copies as well as an eBook, but the standard of production, including editorial and design, remains the same though the cover may sometimes include a few more embellishments. In this scenario, you're paying up to $20 a book for the same content and layout you would receive at the cheap end and you may still have very limited ways of selling or marketing those finished copies.

None of this means that you should never use one of these companies, and nor does it mean that the package approach is intrinsically wrong. But make your decision based on reality, not blind faith. Creating a book isn't difficult but creating a quality book is considerably harder and selling that book effectively is harder still.

HOW TO CHOOSE THE RIGHT PUBLISHING SERVICES BUSINESS FOR YOU

A long list of services can be beguiling, because it makes you feel as though you're getting great value for your money. It may be useful, however, to think about other types of purchases we all make, such as a piece of kitchen equipment or a home appliance. We're drawn in by all the fancy options on offer, yet when we start to use the piece of equipment, we discover that all we really wanted were the core functions.

The same is true when you're choosing a company to help you make your book. Keep your plan firmly in mind and focus on the services that will help you achieve it. Cynicism is your friend. If an offer seems too good to be true, the chances are that *it is,* so don't just accept what you're told. Research carefully, read between the lines and take sensible steps to protect yourself:

- Check user reviews and ask for informed feedback from authors who've successfully funded their own publications.
- Ask questions if there are terms or conditions that are vague or difficult to understand.
- Request a detailed list of the services on offer along with a copy of the company's standard agreement.
- Obtain at least two or three quotes from different companies so that you can compare the alternatives before you make your final decision.
- There are also websites and blogs that alert prospective authors to the dangers of vanity presses masquerading as bona fide publishers. A couple of the best known are an American site called Writer Beware and the Alliance of Independent Authors' rating of self-publishing companies.

Above all, remember that you're paying for the services you need to turn your manuscript into a quality book. The company providing these services doesn't need to have anything to do with your copyright. You should never sign an agreement about which you are uncertain without obtaining expert advice, which you can get through the ASA.

BEST ALTERNATIVES

Before you despair completely, there are alternatives to consider:

Custom publishing

If you have the resources, there are a few service providers, usually using the term custom publisher, who will charge at the upper end of the scale, but who will use experienced publishing staff to create a high-quality book and then work with you to help you sell and market it. Again, it's essential to do your own research, but potential places to start your investigation are Slattery Media and Ventura Press.

EBook only/print on demand

If you only want to publish digitally and feel comfortable in the digital environment, you can load your eBooks onto the major digital retail platforms yourself and manage the process from there. You must bear in mind, however, that in order to access the primary eBook retail platforms you'll have to convert your completed files into ePub (most platforms) and Mobi (for Amazon only, although Amazon have announced they will soon also accept ePub files).

Many of the following companies will do this step for you, although most can also take care of the loading to, and management of, the retail platforms: BookBaby, Draft2Digital (which recently acquired Smashwords), EBook Alchemy, IndieMosh, IngramSpark, and Lulu. Take the time to examine their list of services and then select the options that best suit your goals and capabilities.

Audiobooks

ACX, Amazon's platform for creating audiobooks and then selling them on Audible, iTunes and Amazon, is the largest and most preferred audiobook partner for many authors, but at this stage Australian authors are not eligible to open an account as you must be a resident of the US, UK, Canada or Republic of Ireland. There are, however, other options.

ListenUp, based in the US, offers a range of services from full production of your audiobook through to distribution. As at the beginning of 2022, their average rates are $450 USD for a finished hour of audio, which translates to a cost of $3,150 USD for an average length book – about $4,500 AUD, depending on the exchange rate.

Findaway Voices (recently acquired by Spotify) also offers both production and distribution services. They indicate about $1,500 USD to produce a 50,000-word book, which is about $2,200 AUD.

We'll cover the distribution of audiobooks in more detail in the next section of the guide.

Sales

Regardless of the route that you use, you can make a high-quality book of the same standard as a traditionally published title but selling and marketing it are the next hurdles.

EBOOKS

Digital channels to market are considerably easier to organise than print sales and there are only a handful of major platforms that you should consider including. All of them use a form of digital rights management (DRM), which is a way of protecting your copyright by making the file accessible only to the purchaser.

Amazon

Amazon is hard to ignore in the eBook world because of the degree to which it dominates digital sales in the UK and US. There are two ways in which you can publish your work; general distribution and Kindle Select (KDP Select), which is an exclusive arrangement with Amazon for a minimum of 90 days. If you're unsure what to do, you can register for KDP Select at any time, so there's no need to worry about this when you're initially loading your book.

You will, however, have to make a call about royalty structure: Amazon offers 70% and 30% of retail price royalty options, depending on the price point you select.

Until recently, selling your own print books on Amazon wasn't a viable option for Australian authors, but in 2021 Amazon Australia opened their own print-on-demand facility, so it's worth making sure that you keep up to date on this service.

Rakuten Kobo

Rakuten Kobo has general distribution including Kobo itself, Booktopia and Overdrive, which licenses eBooks into libraries.

Rakuten Kobo offers a free conversion tool that allows any author, or indeed publisher, to convert their manuscript into an EPub file that will be readable as an eBook on all reading devices other than the Kindle. Although there's a range of Kobo readers available, a customer doesn't have to purchase one in order to read a Kobo eBook.

Their website has detailed instructions on how to format your files. The arrangement is non-exclusive, which means that you're free to load your eBook onto as many other platforms as you'd like. Provided you price your eBook at a minimum of $2.99 AUD, you receive 70% of the retail revenue. If you price under that level, your revenue share drops to 45% and if the book were to be public domain (meaning the copyright has expired), the rate would drop to 20%.

Payment is made monthly, 45 days after the month in which you made the sales, but you get paid only if the amount exceeds $50. If payment falls below that, it rolls over to the next month. This can happen only for six months, however. At the end of that period, you're paid everything you've earned so far, even if that total still doesn't reach the minimum.

In April 2020, Rakuten Kobo and Booktopia signed an agreement, which means that your eBook will have good exposure both in Australia and internationally.

Apple Books

Although it makes sense to ensure that your eBook is available on all the major platforms, Apple Books is said to be harder to use than Amazon and is, of course, restricted to Mac OS. IBooks take a 30% commission on each sale and pay monthly, 30 days after the month in which the sale was made. If the payment doesn't reach $30, no payment will be made and the outstanding amount will roll over to the next month.

Barnes & Noble

The Barnes & Noble site has reputedly become more user friendly. Like Kobo, it isn't exclusive. The split of revenue is 70/30 in the author's favour, regardless of the price point. The payment threshold is only $10, under which the amount is rolled over, but, as with Kobo, any money due will be paid out at six months.

Google Play

You need to apply to become part of the Google Books Partner Program. Google Play uses the wholesale pricing model and splits the income 70/30 in your favour. They make the payment 15 days after the end of the month in which the sale was made and the threshold to roll over payment is $100.

If you would prefer not to manage each of these accounts yourself, you can use one of the aggregators listed in the previous section.

AUDIO BOOKS

It's a significant challenge for Australian indie authors that they can't directly distribute their audiobooks to Amazon and Audible via Audiobook Creation Exchange (ACX), but there are a range of options for you to consider when you're ready to sell your audiobook. As with eBooks, the easiest approach is to use an aggregator who can ensure that your audiobook is available for sale on all the major platforms.

If you want your audiobook to be available as a CD as well as a digital download, then a good place to start is BookBaby, where you can produce and distribute your book on CD. These days, it wouldn't be prudent to produce CDs unless you knew there was a market for them and you had a sales channel to connect to that market. In general, however, distribution is for digital audiobooks.

Many of the aggregators listed in the eBook section will also handle distribution/sales for audiobooks, but there are also specialist audio platforms. All have non-exclusive agreements and cover the major platforms, including Audible.

ListenUp pays the author 80% of the royalties it receives from retailers and libraries. There is a $149–$199 USD one-off set-up fee which you don't have to pay if you also produce your book with this company. Audible pays ListenUp a 25% royalty, of which 80% goes to the author, whereas other global platforms will pay a 40–50% royalty, which is split 80/20 in the author's favour.

Findaway Voices has the same financial arrangement as ListenUp and a similar network of platforms.

Although they do partner with a production company, unlike the other two companies mentioned, Author's Republic focuses solely on distribution. The revenue split is 70/30 in the author's favour and, other than Audible, this company generally receives a 50% royalty from their retail partners.

As always, make sure that you carefully research any business you're planning to use, particularly checking reviews from those who've already used the service.

BRICKS AND MORTAR STORES

Accessing bricks and mortar bookshops is considerably more difficult because your options are narrow. Some bookshops will stock self-published titles from local authors, but many have been burnt in the past and will no longer accept books directly from the author. If you have a good relationship with your local bookshop, you could be one of the lucky ones, but you need to understand what's involved:

- The shop will want to take the books on consignment, which means they won't pay you for a book until it's been sold. The risk therefore rests with you.
- They will pay, on average, a 45% discount off the retail price excluding GST. So if your book is retailing at $29.95, that's $27.23 ex GST: the bookshop would pay you $14.97.
- They will expect you to deliver the stock, supply them with a tax invoice and collect any unsold copies.

Even if you can access your local shops, you need to be realistic about the number of books you may sell, which is likely to be no more than 50–100 copies across all the bookshops you're able to contact, unless your book is particularly relevant to your local area. To sell a reasonable volume of books you'll therefore need to access stores throughout Australia and to do that, you'll need a book distributor. These companies have a sales team (usually freelance reps paid on commission) who sell to independent bookstores, some book chains and library wholesalers, but they're unlikely to sell to the discount department stores. They also have a warehouse, and they manage the sales and invoicing into the bookshops, the receipt and storage of stock from the printer, delivery of the stock and credit control.

Distributors charge in one of two ways:

1. A discount off the retail price exclusive of GST, somewhere around 70%, to allow them to give the retailer their 45% to 50% discount and cover their sales and distribution costs
2. They provide a net sales report (the price they receive from the retailer) and then deduct a 25% to 30% commission on those sales.

Currently very few distributors are prepared to represent individual authors, because it's both time-consuming and resource intensive. This is why the ASA set up a distribution service for their members with John Reed Books. If you have a one-off title with high sales potential, or have a proven track record of sales across a range of titles, you could also try Booktopia Publisher Services, Brumby Sunstate (children's and gift book/card sets etc), Peribo, Distributors of Fine Books (largely non-illustrated) and Woodslane (general trade).

It's vital to resolve your distribution before you print.

If you're publishing a children's book, you should also discuss children's book clubs with your distributor. Although these channels are discerning in what they buy, they can place substantial orders. The discount is very high but such an order could help you to generate a bigger and therefore more economical print run.

SHOW ME THE MONEY

Whichever path you follow to self-publication, you must understand the level of investment you're making, and the level of risk. The best way to achieve this is to work out how many copies of your book you'll need to sell to recoup your investment. If you're unlikely to break even, and many author-funded titles don't, you may still decide to go ahead. That's entirely your decision but proceed with your eyes open.

Let's look at an example:

Format:	C format paperback
Retail price print:	$29.95 ($27.22 excluding GST)
Retail price digital:	$9.99
WIP costs:	$3,500
Print costs:	$663 (100 copies)
Total investment:	**$4,163**
Print sales units:	100
Print sales revenue:	$1,497 (retailer buying at 45% discount off retail, $14.97 each)
Digital sales:	200

Digital sales revenue:	$1,271.45
	(70% of $9.08, price ex GST, $6.36)
Total revenue:	**$2,768.45**
(Loss):	**($1,394.55)**

If you didn't want to print more copies, you would need to sell another 220 eBooks at $6.36 to recover all your investment, a total of 100 print copies and 420 eBooks.

But wait, there's more: How have you distributed your print books? If you've used a distributor, you'll have to pay them around 30% of the net revenue from your print sales, reducing your income by a further $450. This would increase your loss to $1,845, meaning that you'd need to sell a total of 280 eBooks to fully recoup your investment. And this is without factoring in the cost of marketing.

Of course, there are many variations that you can cost out, but our example of 100 print sales and almost 300 eBooks is a big ask, given the average sales of new titles.

This is, of course, assuming that all the digital sales are made at full retail price. If you don't have an established name, or you're not writing on a popular subject, it's likely that, at least for some of the time, you'll need to offer your eBook for sale at a lower retail price, somewhere between $3 and $4.99, thus significantly increasing the number of eBooks you'll have to sell to break even.

It's also difficult to break even with an audiobook in the mix. If you have $3,500 production costs, based on a $29.99 retail price and the revenue structure outlined in the sales section, to break even you'd need to sell at least

640 audiobook downloads on the Audible platform or 320 units on the other platforms. If you were selling on all platforms, your break-even would be somewhere in the vicinity of 500 units, because of the dominance of Audible, which pays the lowest royalty rate.

These scenarios demonstrate just how difficult it is to earn back your investment, before you even consider making any profit. They also reveal that, in most circumstances, it is impossible to break even on the high-end packages offered by some service providers. This is why so many people try to minimise their risk by cutting corners. Then it becomes a vicious circle as the quality and appeal of your book are reduced in direct proportion to that cost-cutting. The only escape routes are to either accept that cost recovery is unlikely and invest at a level that you can afford, or boost sales, and therefore revenue, by actively marketing your work.

Discoverability: Marketing and promoting your book

How easy is it for potential readers to find your book?

Searching for a specific title these days is fast and easy. You only need to enter that title into your search engine or one of the major book retail platforms and you'll be able to find and purchase the book with a couple of clicks. The problem begins when you don't know the title, or even that the book exists. Discoverability is all about making it easy for people who are interested in the genre or style of book you've written, to find your title when they're searching for something to read.

Discoverability is a complicated business, and we can't hope to cover everything you need in this guide. There's an enormous amount of information available online and an unlimited number of courses that you can do, but, as ever, ensure that the resources you're using are reliable. Much of this information is free, so if you're being asked to pay, do your due diligence: you should be able to learn the basics without any financial outlay.

THE BASICS

Quality design

A book's cover design is the first thing that a prospective customer sees, and if it doesn't grab their attention, or is a beautiful cover but fails to accurately represent the content, it won't serve you well.

Don't fall into the trap of thinking that if the content is good enough, the book will sell itself: quality cover design is an important element of discoverability. Conduct research on other books, especially the bestsellers, in your genre in both bricks and mortar bookshops and online so that you can give your designer a detailed and knowledgeable brief.

Define your customer

As part of your publishing plan you'll already have defined your target market. The more you know about your potential customers, the more effectively you can position and promote your book. Some additional questions to consider include:

- Which influencers do your readers follow?
- Which other authors do they like to read? What are some of their favourite books?
- Where do they get their book news and information?
- Which book clubs or literary events do they go to, if any?
- Which social media channels do they prefer?
- What are their favourite blogs, podcasts, radio shows and so on?

This information is essential in order to plan marketing and publicity activities that are likely to reach your customer.

Accurate metadata

To the uninitiated, metadata can sound intimidating, but it simply means attaching words (often termed keywords) and phrases to your work that will help people to find your book/s when they're searching the internet or retailer sites. This data is important because few people outside your immediate circle will know that you've even published a book so they won't be searching by title. They're much more likely to be searching by topics and words that relate to their areas of interest, for example 'WW2 biographies'

If you can therefore attach data to your title that's likely to catch the attention of your target market, you'll make it much easier for them to find your book.

All the basic metadata is entered when you apply for your ISBN and barcode, including title, subtitle and series name if appropriate, author, author biography, publication date, ISBN and book description. It's critical that this data is consistent and accurate, so resist the temptation to keep making changes to any of these areas, most particularly your biography or the description of your book.

We then come to categories, which detail the subject matter of your book, e.g. Biography & Autobiography/Aviation & Nautical. If you're using a service provider to make your book, they may have a drop-down list of available categories when you're loading all your title details, which will guide you through the process of selecting the right one/ones. If you're going it alone you'll need to ensure that you attach the right categories to your book. Unfortunately, there have been two different sets of categories: BISAC, the subject categories used in the US, and BIC, which are used in the UK. These two groups have been working for some years on combining the codes into one category listing called Thema, which is now starting to phase in. At this stage, it's still wise to allocate categories from all three codes. You can find them here:

BIC	https://ns.editeur.org/bic_categories
BISAC	https://bisg.org/page/BISAC Selection
Thema	https://ns.editeur.org/thema/en

This isn't as difficult as it sounds. All three have listings and you simply choose the first category code, which will be a high-level classification such as fiction, and when you click on that you'll be able to add a further code that defines the genre and then the subject matter.

Once you've coded your book, you need to think carefully about 4–6 *keywords* that describe your work. Selecting the right words will help potential customers find your title if they're searching for one of those terms. To do this, consider how someone might search for, and find, a book like yours. For instance, if you've written a crime novel detailing the investigation of a crime by police, you can use a phrase like 'police procedural'.

Remember that keywords, despite their name, do not have to be single words. In fact, best practice would involve using a combination of short keywords, and long-tail keywords (longer and more specific), or phrases made up of three or more keywords.

There are a number of tools available that can help you to select the most effective keywords. Many of them focus on Amazon, but the principles of keywords remain the same throughout the internet. These tools include Google Trends, which allows you to compare the popularity of different search terms, Kindlepreneur's article 'How to Select Kindle Keywords', and Jane Friedman's 'Optimising Your Books for Amazon Keyword Search'.

For search engine optimisation (SEO), you'll want to make sure that you use these keywords in the book description and in all the promotional and marketing copy that you may write. Not to be confused with search engine marketing (SEM), which is paid advertising, SEO is the free process by which you can improve the discoverability of your product or website on a search engine like Google or Bing.

There are many different elements of SEO, and plenty of information about it is freely available online, but the most important factor is ensuring that all the content you're producing about your work uses keywords that target your prospective customers.

Website

Most 'experts' maintain that it's important for an author, particularly a self-funded one, to have a website, and in principle this is correct. There's an expectation these days that searching for a business or a name will reveal a website, or at least a blog, Facebook page or LinkedIn profile.

The benefit of a website is that it makes it convenient for people to find information about you and your work all in one place. However, websites are discoverable only if you're using the right keywords, and the content is refreshed and updated, drawing new audiences to you. This is because search engines like Google prioritise regularly updated websites in the search results over websites that have remained static for months.

Because books take a long time to write and produce, many author websites aren't dynamic – the content changes irregularly and infrequently. If you're going to invest in a website, you'll want to consider how you can regularly refresh the content, such as incorporating a blog, or a news section that will allow you to post a variety of content suited to your core audience.

Many author websites are terrible, with poor design and out of date content. But the new, free or inexpensive platforms now available make it possible to create a beautiful site quickly and economically. Three of the most popular and user-friendly are Squarespace, Wix and Wordpress.

Many people with quite basic computer skills can develop their own site, but you can get someone else to do it for a modest charge. The beauty of these sites is that it's easy to add and take away material and plug in a blog, keeping the site fresh and engaging, with good SEO. It's also simple to provide links to online retailers and your local bookshop so that you don't have to manage book sales.

So, a website is a good thing, but only if it's a dynamic, professional site that helps drive traffic to you and your book.

MARKETING AND PUBLICITY PLAN

Even if you've produced a high-quality book, with great metadata supported by an enticing website, you still have to do everything you can to make your prospective customers aware that your book is being published. Well before the publication date, you'll want to draw up a marketing and publicity plan, which summarises key information and puts a clear map in place for your activities. This plan should include:

- ***Your objective:*** consider a specific and measurable goal for your marketing and publicity plan, e.g. sell 50 books in six months, or get 15 pre-orders before publication day
- ***A key message:*** this should be simple, clear and relate to your plan objective. It should express what your prospective customer can expect from your book and include a call to action. For example, 'Outback crime written by Australia's most infamous homicide detective. Pre-order now'
- ***Marketing channels:*** identify your target market to establish the best channels to get your message out there. These may include social media channels, newsletters, blogs and so on. Be sure to select the channels best suited to your target market
- ***Resources:*** you need to be realistic about your budget, and the amount of time you have to invest in your marketing and publicity activities
- ***A calendar of marketing activities:*** these may include paid advertising, promotions or discounts, merchandise such as bookmarks, and so on
- ***A calendar of publicity activities:*** publicity is about generating free word-of-mouth coverage for your book. Publicity activities may include sending sell sheets or advance reading copies of your book to bloggers, influencers or media outlets, or arranging podcast interviews.

You'll want to adapt the plan as time passes, particularly as you evaluate the activities that are producing the best results, but having a calendar of activity will help you to build momentum towards your publication date and for the months afterwards.

BUILDING A COMMUNITY: SOCIAL MEDIA, BLOGS AND MAILING LISTS

Building a community and author brand is the necessary foundation of all of your promotional activities. If you're a non-fiction writer with a specialist area of expertise, chances are that you'll already have contacts within the community interested in the subject matter of your book. If you write fiction or children's books, you may not have yet established such an audience, so you'll need to start building this base well ahead of your publication date. The most successful self-published authors work very hard at developing these networks.

Where to begin if you are starting from scratch? First, choose which channel or channels you will use to build your community, by researching the one/s your prospective customers are likely to use, and where your strengths lie. For example, if you've written a YA book and you enjoy creating video content, you might choose to use TikTok. You don't need to be on every social media channel, have a blog and send out a newsletter. Instead of trying to do everything poorly, pick one or more channels where you can excel with the time and resources you have available.

Your next step is research, starting with the books that already appeal to your target market. Study the authors of those titles carefully. Check out their websites, their social media posts and subscribe to their blogs. Investigate the communities they're a part of: Who are the influencers, bloggers and reviewers? Who do they engage with? What are the key topics of conversation?

Once you've identified groups interested in your genre or subject matter, it's time to follow and start engaging with them. Interact with their content and actively participate in those communities. You'll want to do this well ahead of publication, so that by the time you're ready to start promoting your book, you'll have established your credibility.

This is an important point: you should enter online communities thinking about what you have to offer, not just what you can get out of them. No one likes to feel used, so overt spruiking of your book without genuine involvement is likely to backfire. Discuss issues that are relevant to your audience, ask questions and create dialogue with interested readers. It's ideas, information and interaction that will draw interest, not constant ads exhorting people to buy your book.

Newsletters are one of the most significant ways for an author to reach their audience. This is because, unlike social media, you don't need your audience to be online at the right time to see what you post, or have to rely on the algorithm to favour your account. A newsletter will be sitting in your reader's inbox for them to read, any time it suits. It does, though, take a substantial amount of time and consistent effort to build a mailing list, and you must have some kind of platform through which your target audience can find and subscribe to your content.

Once you've established a platform, you can direct your followers to subscribe to your newsletter. Please note that you must *not* manually subscribe anyone to your newsletter or blog without their explicit agreement: not only is it illegal, but it will damage your credibility. You must also always provide a clear link to an unsubscribe button so that anyone can opt out as easily as they opted in.

SECURING BOOK REVIEWS

One of the best ways to spread the word about your book is via reviews. These, however, have to be genuine: audiences are savvy and won't take kindly to lack of authenticity.

There are plenty of free publicity activities you can undertake to garner reviews for your book, such as sending a sell sheet and a reading copy of your book to key influencers in your community. You can also use paid services, like NetGalley, which, for a fee, promotes digital review copies of your book to their subscribers – librarians, booksellers, educators and reviewers. It's not cheap, but it can be an excellent way to attract expert reviews and raise the profile of your work.

Do your due diligence when it comes to paid reviewing services and pay attention to what exactly they offer. Not all of them guarantee that your book will be reviewed, and none of them guarantee a positive review.

You can find a list of services on the ASA's website.

PAID ADVERTISING

Word of mouth is still the best generator of book sales, but you can also target your core audience with paid advertising on social media and some of the retail platforms selling your book. Check out all your options, from Twitter promotional posts through to advertisements in newsletters, but remember to always keep your target market at the front of your mind because your subject matter and the preferences of your audience will help you work out which channels will be the most effective.

The ASA provides resources on marketing and promotion, including some helpful templates for press releases and publicity plans. There's also a considerable amount of free information online about how to effectively advertise on social media channels, Google, Amazon and so on, but make sure to be discerning.

You must also pay attention to the retail platforms that are selling your book. Research the many articles available online on how best to maximise these promotional opportunities and consider lowering the price point for a set period, to give sales a boost.

Much of this will require trial and error and watching what other people do. Identify the bestselling authors in your category and observe how they manage their pricing. And listen to the experts. Mark Dawson, an enormously successful self-published British thriller writer, has a site dedicated to helping indie authors build sustainable careers from their writing, including a host of useful resources, some of which are available free.

When you actually release your book onto the market, make sure that every link you've established is current since you want to make the most of any hype surrounding publication. One of the advantages of managing your own publication, however, is that, unlike traditional publishers, you can continue to provide marketing support for as long as you want. It may be at a more modest level, but it's possible to keep igniting interest many months after the book is first released.

MARKETING SUMMARY

The way people search for information has a strong correlation to age. Because they're digital natives, younger generations have an ease and familiarity with social media that older, two-finger typists can never hope to emulate. Remember, though, that most of us drive a car without having any understanding of what lies beneath the bonnet. You may need help navigating the processes involved in digital marketing, but the basic principles remain constant: a high-quality book with a stand-out cover and blurb, and interesting, pertinent ancillary content that is continually refreshed and updated.

You do need to keep at it, however. There's a huge range of competing work available and your audience's attention can stray quickly. Keep your marketing plan to hand at all times and fine-tune it based on the responses you receive to your various activities. You'll make mistakes, but the beauty of digital marketing is that much of it is measurable If you change the price of your book or pay for a social media promotional spot, you can see the response and assess whether it was worthwhile, bearing in mind that building awareness of your work may not always translate directly to an increase in revenue. Be generous about supporting others in your community: the stronger that group becomes, the higher the chances are that everyone's sales will benefit and the more likely they'll be to support you in return.

Continue to read and research. Watch what successful authors are doing and try to emulate their patterns. Ask your audience for feedback and listen to it carefully and do everything you can to learn and increase your knowledge. It takes time, and your first book may fall below your expectations, but if you execute your marketing plan well, you'll have considerable information and experience that you can apply to your next books.

Mark Dawson now has more than 2 million downloads of his books under his belt. In his view, 'It's an amazing time to be a writer. If you have the skill and the determination, you can build a career like this, too.'

Common mistakes and how to avoid them

LACK OF MARKET RESEARCH

You may write in isolation, but you certainly won't be publishing in isolation. It's critical that you research and understand which books are selling strongly in your target market and try to identify the common factors. Look at how they're formatted and designed, not because you want to copy them, but because the common themes will show you what your audience is looking for. Also check the page extent of the books in your category. If the average is 75,000 words, a common length in fiction, and your novel is 130,000 words, you're immediately reducing your book's appeal if you fail to edit it down to a more acceptable length.

POOR COVER DESIGN

At the risk of repetition, your book not only has to be a good read, it also has to be well presented. This means an eye-catching, compelling cover that is genre appropriate, along with an effective blurb.

NO EDITING OR BAD EDITING

Self-editing isn't an option. Of course you want to get your manuscript into the best possible shape before you publish, but you're too close to your own work to pick up the things that will stand out to a professional editor, including:

- Grammar and spelling errors
- Overuse of certain words and phrases
- Repetition
- Overwriting
- Plot and structural issues.

Your readers may not always be able to articulate why they're not enjoying the book, but they'll rapidly form an impression of lack of care and sloppiness and will make this clear in their reviews.

LACK OF INDUSTRY UNDERSTANDING

Every industry has its unspoken rules and publishing is no exception. In bricks and mortar stores, this is even more significant. You need to know how far ahead of the publication date the bookseller must make their buying decision, the material they require to make that decision and the all-important buying terms, including the level of discount and right of return, that they expect. You must also research the peak selling times for your genre, in both print and digital formats, so you know what types of books are released when, and why.

INCORRECT FORMATTING

It would be helpful if every digital platform worked within the same parameters, but they don't. You therefore need to ensure that if you're managing your eBook yourself, you design it with as much care as if it were in print, observing the file requirements specified by each retail platform.

POOR METADATA

The term can seem very intimidating to the uninitiated but, as we've seen, it's really just the words and phrases you use to describe both yourself and the book you've written.

The book blurb/description is a particularly important aspect of the metadata. Authors often don't make a good job of writing these, because they find it difficult to both summarise the plot and entice the reader. But apart from the cover, this short description is the only basis on which readers can make their buying decision. Study good blurbs of authors in your genre, but if you still feel at sea send your editor the points you'd like to cover and have them do the job for you.

INCORRECT PRICING

This is a complicated aspect of the digital world. Pricing too high will alienate your potential buyers, but price too low and you'll give the impression that your work is below standard. Print books are considerably easier because they've become locked into certain set price brackets, depending on the genre, length and format.

Once again research is king. Understand the pricing range in your category of eBooks, particularly in the better selling titles, and then try to establish when those titles are promoted, and to what levels. It's fine to price slightly under market rates if you're a first-time author, but if the prevailing prices are between $9.99 and $12.99, you don't want to release your book at $4.99.

INADEQUATE MARKETING SUPPORT

You can write the best book in the world, but if no one knows it's available, sales will be minimal. This is the reason that authors join book groups and use beta readers, as these people can form the base of their marketing community. But no one wants to use or abuse relationships by bombarding family and friends with marketing messages, so if you have no experience in social media and marketing, you must upskill. The best social media marketing feels authentic and managing it yourself allows you to really enthuse potential purchasers with your knowledge and passion for your genre and your book.

Another common mistake is not thinking through a marketing plan early on. Remember, you're the publisher and, like a publisher, you need to plan your marketing and publicity well ahead of publication.

CHILDREN'S ILLUSTRATED BOOKS

Picture books deserve a special mention here, because of the complications that can occur when two people are involved: the author and illustrator. In a typical scenario, the author will have written the text and then sourced an illustrator, in much the same way as a publisher does in a traditional arrangement. But in order to avoid future conflicts, the way in which the arrangement will operate must be agreed before the illustrator starts work.

The easiest and least problematic structure is for the author to commission the illustrator under an assignment of copyright agreement given that most authors are not set up to pay royalties and provide sales statements. In this scenario the author sets out a detailed brief for the illustrator, including the number of illustrations, the size (e.g. half-page, full-page or double-page spreads), whether they are black and white and/or colour, the size and medium of delivery of the final work and so on. When the extent of the work has been agreed, a set fee is negotiated and an agreement is drawn up, clarifying that the illustrator has assigned the copyright in the illustrations to the author for the specified sum. A refresher fee can be included in the event that the book sells more than an agreed number of copies.

If the illustrator isn't willing to give up their copyright, a copyright licence can be negotiated. The same detailed brief about the content is prepared, along with clarification concerning the licence:

- ***The term of the licence:*** how long does the agreement last?
- ***The territories that are being included:*** Australia only or world rights?
- ***The formats that are included:*** hardback, paperback, digital, audio etc.
- ***The licence fee:*** upfront one-off sum, or yearly payment or royalties on sales?

It is essential that these negotiations are then captured in a written agreement that is signed by both parties. The ASA has contract templates that cover both scenarios.

Next steps

Writing is a solitary occupation, but so is self-funded publishing. Unlike traditionally published authors, you must navigate the complexities of making, selling and marketing your book on your own. This can be lonely and, at times, bewildering. It calls for courage.

Many self-funding authors take this step because they hope that if they secure a strong level of sales on their own, this could attract the attention of a publisher. This is a double-edged sword. If your book sells strongly and you've built a community around your work, there's a chance that this will attract publisher attention and if they consider that you're a writer worthy of further investment, they may well beat a path to your door. But if this does happen, they're much more likely to be interested in your future work, rather than in republishing your existing title.

There are exceptions to this. The publisher could believe that your book hasn't reached its full potential and could be interested in repackaging and republishing your title in order to maximise those sales. But this is rare. On the whole, once you've published your book, that's it. It's been made available and with so many manuscripts on offer, publishers will have little interest in trying to revive books that haven't sold well on their first release. It's risky to produce your own work in order to attract publisher attention, unless you know that your title has a real chance of making a strong impact.

Some of you will have a wonderful experience. Your sales will meet or exceed your expectations, your share of revenue will be considerably more than a traditional publishing arrangement and you'll feel encouraged to build on your success with your next book. This scenario can and does happen and although it's difficult to secure accurate numbers, many authors, particularly in the genres mentioned earlier, are generating steady and, more rarely, high incomes, from their self-published work. If you're one of them, there's little reason to change course.

For most of you, however, this won't be the case. You'll see maybe a couple of hundred eBooks and get a handful of reviews, but you're unlikely to cover your costs and may well be left feeling disheartened. Your next steps will depend on your motivation to continue writing and publishing. Having your book released may be enough. If you published to support your business, as is the case with many self-funding authors, your book can serve many useful purposes other than the revenue that it generates. Likewise, if you wanted to produce your book primarily for family and friends, you may well have achieved your goal.

The next steps are up to you, but remember that *if you change nothing, nothing will change.* If you want to give self-publishing another go, try to stand back and objectively assess what you did right, and where you may have gone wrong.

- Was your cover right for your genre and was it good enough?

- Did your blurb capture attention?
- Was your metadata up-to-date and consistent?
- Were your sales disappointing because readers reviewed your book poorly, or were those sales poor because no one knew you'd published it?

Honest assessment will help you develop a better plan for your next book if you want to continue to write and publish. Try to upskill where you can, particularly in developing your writing and enhancing the discoverability of your book. Regardless of how a book has come into being, the chances of your first attempt being a runaway success are small, so the advice is the same for self-published writers as it is for those who have traversed the traditional path. If your work is of publishable standard and your love of writing feeds your soul, then you will have no choice but to keep writing.

> *'If you are a real writer, then just surrender to the writer's life, all of it, even the bad stuff. When you do that, the beauty appears: the peace, the meaning, the joy, the fulfillment, the sense that you are doing what you were born to do and what could be better, in the end, than that?'*
>
> Lauren B. Davis, author

PART 4

PART 4

Supplementing your income

For many, if not most writers, it's difficult to make sufficient income from publishing alone, so you need to think about ways of supplementing your income, by drawing on your skills in different ways. Lending rights and Copyright Agency payments are a helpful start, but there are other options.

Grants

There are many potential sources of grants, but three of the most significant for writers and illustrators are those managed by the Australia Council for the Arts, the Cultural Fund managed by the Copyright Agency and your state government's arts funding body. The ASA offers a list of the major grant options available on their website.

Public speaking and events, including school and/or library appearances

This is particularly relevant for children's and adult non-fiction writers, both to generate income from speaking fees and to build a community for future book sales. For guidance on payment rates for public speaking and events, the ASA publishes recommended rates of pay, which you can find on its website.

School and library appearances are an important source of income for children's and YA authors, particularly around the Children's Book Council of Australia's Book Week. You'll need a Working with Children check in the state/territory in which you work.

If you write children's books and are interested in finding work as a speaker in schools, the Primary English Teaching Association Australia (PETAA) has published a guide for authors and illustrators visiting and presenting in schools. It covers the most important information you'll need, including English in the curriculum, school finances and what a school expects from an author. You'll find the guide on PETAA's website.

There are several speaker agencies that represent authors to speak in schools and libraries. Each has their own criteria for the authors they choose to represent, and most are state based, rather than national.

If you're keen to become part of the 'celebrity' speaking network, there are many speaker bureaus that manage this type of work, mostly for corporate audiences. Before you join their list, they'll want to see evidence of your success as a speaker in schools and at public events. As always, research thoroughly before making any commitments. Study the agency's talent list and if you have a personal connection to one of the speakers, try to find out their opinion of the business. If you have a publisher, their publicity department will know some of the best agencies and may be able to assist with an introduction.

Festivals

The ASA offers a comprehensive listing of major festivals in Australia. Although all festivals have a dedicated shop selling the most relevant titles by each participating author, the primary reason that authors aspire to attend these events is exposure to an audience with a passion for books and reading.

It's difficult, however, to provide advice on how you can go about getting an invitation. A few festivals, such as the Melbourne Writers' Festival, have a form on their website, and other websites include a small piece about submissions, but overall, authors are invited at the discretion of the festival director. Authors are selected on the basis of, among other things,

- Their relevance to the theme of the festival, which usually changes from year to year
- The profile and reviews of their book
- Their 'reach' in terms of their social media platform
- Their ability to engage an audience.

The best way of securing an invitation as a festival guest is to generate as much positive publicity for your book as possible, including being willing to speak to any group that shows interest in your work.

Literary Prizes

There are many literary prizes offered to Australian writers and illustrators, including pre-publication awards for emerging authors and post-publication awards for published books. You can find a non-exhaustive list of prizes on the ASA's website.

Make sure that you read the conditions of entry carefully. Each prize has different criteria, including whether they allow self-published authors to enter their work, and many charge an entry fee. If you're traditionally published, your publisher will decide which books they wish to enter for which prizes, but if you've funded your own work, do your best to match your book to the most suitable prizes. You can waste considerable time and money making ineffective submissions.

Freelance Writing

This is easier to secure if you're a non-fiction writer, but many literary journals will take poetry and short story submissions. You can find a list of Australian journals on the ASA website. The ASA recommends you always ensure that you'll be paid for your work.

Mentoring

If you have an established writing career, mentoring can be a very rewarding way of passing on your knowledge and earning additional income. The ASA offers mentorships to all published and unpublished writers and illustrators with a work in progress, and many writers' organisations offer mentoring schemes.

Workshops

The ASA, and other writers' organisations offer an extensive range of workshops to aspiring and established writers, many of which are facilitated by authors.

Start by thinking carefully about the skills, experience and knowledge you have that may benefit other writers. These could be related to your writing, e.g. how to conduct research if you're a non-fiction writer of history, but they could equally relate to other roles that have formed part of your career, such as business skills, organising your time appropriately or writing grant applications.

When you have identified an area or areas where you believe you could make a worthwhile contribution, write a short precis of the way in which you would conduct a workshop. In many ways, it's similar to preparing a publisher submission for your book, so try and include the following:

- A strong title
- A brief two-sentence description of the topics you'll cover
- An outline of the workshop which fleshes out those topics
- The length of the workshop (an hour, half a day etc.)
- The target audience
- Any information that you can provide for the participants to take away.

Once you're happy with your document, prepare a cover letter and send this and your proposal to any organisation that matches your target group. Many will be seeking fresh faces to bring to their training programs, and a strong proposal should at least open the door to a conversation.

For guidance on payment rates, remember that the ASA publishes recommended rates of pay which you can find on its website.

PART 5

PART 5

Industry organisations

When building a career as an author, here is a list of national industry organisations you should know about:

Australian Society of Authors

www.asauthors.org

The ASA is the national professional association for writers and illustrators. It provides a wide range of services, including an advice service, a professional development program, mentoring and FAQs. Important resources include:

- The ASA's Guide to the Australian Book Industry
- *More Than Words; Writing, Aboriginal and Torres Strait Islander Culture and Copyright in Australia* for guidance on ICIP best practice
- Contract templates between authors and publishers, authors and literary agents and authors and illustrators (for indie publishing)

The ASA also regularly runs Literary Speed Dating, a unique opportunity for you to pitch your work directly to Australian publishers and agents. Illustrators may showcase their work on the ASA's portfolio website, The ASA Style File: www.asastylefile.com

Authors Legal

www.authorslegal.org

Authors Legal is a subsidiary of the ASA and a non-profit law firm dedicated to low-cost legal advice to Australian writers and illustrators. Authors Legal offers a contract review service for advice on publishing, agency or distribution agreements.

Arts Law Centre of Australia

www.artslaw.com.au

Arts Law centre offers free or low cost legal advice to creators as well as contract templates and information sheets (for example, on Defamation).

ATO

www.ato.gov.au/business/GST

For advice on registering for GST see the ATO website.

Australian Book Designers Association

www.abda.com.au

The Australian Book Designers Association supports Australian book designers and has a useful searchable member directory.

Australian Booksellers Association

www.booksellers.org.au

The Australian Booksellers Association is the national association for booksellers and supports its members through education and training, marketing support and technical advice. It has launched a buying group to optimise terms with publishers.

Australian Business Register

www.abr.gov.au/business-super-funds-charities/applying-abn

For advice on applying for an ABN, see the Australian Business Register website.

Australian Copyright Council

www.copyright.org.au

The Australian Copyright Council provides many useful fact sheets and publications answering all copyright-related questions.

Australian Library and Information Association

www.alia.org.au

The Australian Library and Information Association (ALIA) is the peak professional organisation for the Australian library and information services sector.

Australian Literary Agents Association

www.austlitagentsassoc.com

The Literary Agents Association provides a non-exhaustive list of Australian literary agencies. It also sets out a Code of Practice for its members.

Australian Publishers Association

www.publishers.asn.au

The Australian Publishers Association (APA) is the national representative body for the Australian publishing industry. It makes available a searchable directory of APA member companies.

Copyright Agency

www.copyright.com.au

Copyright Agency is the collecting society for Australian writers and illustrators. It collects fees and distributes royalties to its members for the reuse of text and images. Copyright Agency manages the educational and government statutory licence schemes and you must join as a member to be eligible for payment in the event your work is copied in schools and universities. Membership is free.

First Nations Australian Writers Network

www.fnawn.com.au

The First Nations Australia Writers' Network (FNAWN), is a national advocacy and resources service for Aboriginal and/or Torres Strait Islander writers, poets and storytellers.

Institute of Professional Editors

www.iped-editors.org

The Institute of Professional Editors (IPEd) is the professional association for Australian and New Zealand editors. It offers a useful search directory to help you find an editor who is a professional member of IPED.

MEAA

www.meaa.org/

MEAA is the union and industry advocate for creative professionals.

Office for the Arts

www.arts.gov.au/funding-and-support/lending-rights

The Office for the Arts administers Public and Educational Lending Rights.

SCWBI

www.scbwiaustralianz.com/, www.australiawest.scbwi.org/

The Society of Children's Book Writers and Illustrators has a membership partnership offer with the ASA and not only has a showcase for illustrators, but a very useful handbook that is available to all members.

Sources

The lines quoted on pages 11-12 are from an interview with Ruuf Wangersen in 'The Creative Process & Publishing I - How to get published' by M. Bijman, published on sevencircumstances.com on 7 September 2018.

The lines quoted on page 43 are from *Stet: An Editor's Life* by Diana Athill (Granta, London 2021).

The lines quoted on page 197 are from an interview with Lauren B. Davis in 'Lauren B. Davis' by Jon Winokur, published on advicetowriters.com on 25 February 2014.